THE 8 MASTER KEYS
TO HEALING WHAT HURTS
for the Sensitive Person
© Rue Anne Hass 2006

Contact Rue Hass: Rue@IntuitiveMentoring.com

IntuitiveMentoring.com

References:
Gary Craig's comprehensive website: EmoFree.com
Resources: EFTBooks.com for Books, Tele-Classes, Audios, CDs, DVDs and other EFT materials

For a wealth of information on the sensitive temperament, read my book *This is Where I Stand: the Power and Gift of Being Sensitive,* available on my website. You will find information about the Idealist-Healer/Highly Sensitive Temperament, and using EFT for healing the issues that can arise for such a person.

Go to: IntuitiveMentoring.com/publications.html

Designed, constructed by Angela Treat Lyon
and published by
/UT &RONT 0RODUCTIONS
Kailua, Hawaii
Lyon@Lyon-Art.com

THE 8 MASTER KEYS

TO HEALING WHAT HURTS

for the Highly Sensitive Person

BY
RUE ANNE HASS, M.A.

Foreword by Nancy Selfridge, M.D.

Inside everyone
is a great shout of joy
waiting to be born.

David Whyte
from **The House of Belonging**

CONTENTS

Names of all clients have been changed to ensure privacy

❋ ❋ ❋

Profoundly light-hearted strategies for unsticking stuck stuff

FOREWORD

Nancy Selfridge, M.D. is currently Chief of the Integrative Medicine and Wellness Clinic of Group Health Cooperative HMO in Madison, Wisconsin.

A Neurobiological Model for Fibromyalgia

Presently, the conventional medical model frames fibromyalgia as a syndrome diagnosis. As such, it is simply a name applied to a set of symptoms, primarily pain, and the finding of tender spots on examination occurring in a patient for whom no other explanation exists for this state of being.

In many ways, fibromyalgia is like so many other diseases in our Western medical history. Our understanding of the pathophysiology of this disorder is reliant on an exquisite understanding of the physiology of pain and pain perception, the effects of trauma and stress on the brain, and the ways the emotions are translated into the physiology of symptoms.

 In fact, we are still in the infancy of exploration of these complex processes and, therefore, a complete understanding of how someone with FM gets sick and stays sick eludes us.

As I suffered through my own fibromyalgia symptoms over many years, I remained convinced that this was a problem with my central nervous system and I was reasonably certain that it had been brought about by stress/trauma (in my case, the intensity of my medical training and also a difficult marriage). Still, there was nothing in my medical training that prepared me for understanding and managing my own symptoms, though I really did try about everything that conventional medicine had to offer.

Fortunately, I was introduced to the work of John Sarno, MD, a physiatrist at the Rusk Institute of Rehabilitation, who posited that chronic back pain, and likely all chronic pain, has an emotional base of unresolved rage even when a person is functioning without specific psychological impairment (1). In the words of Dr. Scaer, a gifted neurologist, chronic pain, including FM, is a circumstance where the "body bears the burden" of mental stress and trauma (2).

When I was ready to accept that my FM symptoms might be the neurological equivalent of emotional burden and trauma, and I began focusing on emotion rather than my physical suffering, my physical symptoms evaporated!

Interestingly, I never achieved any physical relief from any of the years of psychotherapy that I did, but this simple association and its complete acceptance in my mind was sufficient.

In essence my thinking shifted from assuming that something awful was happening to my body, to wondering what troublesome emotion was "talking" to me in this form of pain.

After I "healed," I began forming, to the best of my ability, a rudimentary pathophysiology model for FM and sharing this with patients, fine tuning the model as needed to fit the variety of experiences I was hearing in patient histories and also reading about. I noted that almost all of my FM patients where temperamentally similar to me—very sensitive people—and I started asking people if they identified with the traits described by Elaine Aron, PhD, in her books about highly sensitive people (3). Most could readily see themselves in this description.

Of those who had ever taken a Myers Briggs personality test, most were "intuitive feeling" types, also described by David Keirsey, PhD, as "idealist" (4). It seemed as though a certain temperament, or way of being in the world and processing information, might predispose a person to developing chronic physical symptoms when stressed or traumatized. It is an idea yet to be proven, but in my clinical practice it still holds true.

So, what might be actually happening in the brain and body of the FM patient, and what is the scientific support for this?

First, it appears that a sensitive temperament is fertile ground for the development of this disease, almost a "risk factor," you might say.

Then, in nearly all FM patients, there is a stress or trauma (large or small) or a stressful period of time that serves as a forerunner and trigger for the FM symptoms.

The stress/trauma can be physical, mental, emotional or environmental, and in my practice has been as varied as accidents, difficult childbirth, surgery, a significant illness, toxic exposure (such as carbon monoxide), loss of a loved one or a job, a period of too much work, a difficult relationship at home or work, the illness of a loved one, unrelenting financial stress, the intensity of school and studies, lack of adequate sleep, too much caretaking, not enough time for self care for any reason, etc.

After the initiating stress, symptoms start and include pain, fatigue, sleep problems, mood problems, mental fogging, digestive problems, and evidence of autonomic dysfunction such as irritable bladder and fainting. The symptoms vary in location and are unpredictable in their severity. In this respect, they seldom have a pattern that makes any sense, making them even harder to manage. Many people have trouble maintaining a predictable and reliable work schedule, but only 1/3 actually are classified as disabled.

From scientific research, we know that there is abnormal activity in the brain in certain prefrontal cortical areas in response to painful stimuli, that there are abnormal levels of peptides in the brain (chemicals that communicate between brain and body), that there is a deranged pituitary hypothalamic axis mediating the body's endocrine system, but none of these findings has, as yet, emerged as pathognomonic, or diagnostic, for the disease.

In essence, though, it appears that there is a dysregulation of multiple

Profoundly light-hearted strategies for unsticking stuck stuff

body functions, including pain perception, as the net result of this nervous system insult.

Conventional approaches to pain seem not to be helpful, and even therapeutic doses of narcotic pain medication rarely control the FM pain. Perhaps this is because the areas of the brain responsible for FM allodynia (pain amplification) have no opiate receptors. Nonetheless, until we have a better understanding of normal brain function and how FM actually deviates from normal, we will likely be unable to create a "magic bullet" for this disease in the conventional allopathic model.

Ultimately, in my experience, some patients were like me, getting better simply with understanding and accepting a model for their disease that linked the physical symptoms with emotional experience and trauma.

I worked with patients on journaling and simple cognitive exercises to reinforce this idea. However, some patients would find this model easy to accept and still did not have much symptom relief with these exercises.

Thanks to Rue, I was introduced to the *Emotional Freedom Techniques* and energy psychology, which I believe is a breakthrough for the treatment of trauma and post-traumatic stress disorder, and, as such, a treatment for the trauma that appears to induce FM. In fact, many patients achieve remarkable relief for their painful symptoms with EFT.

Under Rue's guidance, foundational beliefs are explored along with the initiating traumas and their deepest meanings. EFT is applied to all aspects of the thoughts, sensations and emotions associated with this exploration, and the FM symptoms improve.

What might be happening here? It is my belief that the areas of the brain that appear to be affected by FM in recent MRI studies are fairly resistant to "quieting" with purely cognitive activity—such as thinking and talking.

Instead, there seems to be an energetic influence from EFT and other therapies like EMDR (Eye Movement Desensitization and Reprocessing), and also with the left prefrontal activation of a meditation practice, that may have a dampening or corrective effect on the problematic prefrontal cortical activity of FM.
It has become apparent to me that FM patients are like "canaries in the coal mine," responding to our stressful culture and environment with real illness and debilitation.

There is nothing about this response that is factitious, nor evidence of psychological disease or bad character. This disorder demands an expansion of our understanding of stress and disease.

As my own awareness of the multiple stressors we are exposed to increases, I expand my counseling of my sensitive FM patients to include diet and nutrition to avoid inflammation and illness, supplements to correct nutritional deficiencies and diligent counseling about stress management strategies and interventions.

Most of all, I give permission to patients to live for their own hearts' desires. I encourage them to explore their limiting beliefs and to honor their sensitive temperaments. It is this latter path that will best help the sensitive soul from becoming sick again.

Nancy Selfridge
Madison, Wisconsin - February, 2006

1. Sarno, John. The Mindbody Prescription: Healing the Body, Healing the Pain. New York: Warner Books, 1998.
   _____. The Divided Mind: Epidemic of Mind Body Disorders. New York: Regan Books, 2006
2. Scaer, Robert C. The Body Bears the Burden. New York: Haworth Medical Press, 2001
3. Aron, Elaine. The Highly Sensitive Person. New York: Broadway Books, 1996
4. Keirsey, David. Please Understand Me II. Del Mar, California: Prometheus Nemesis Publications, 1998

❉ ❉ ❉ ❉ ❉

1
HEALING WHAT HURTS WITH EFT

1: SOME BEFORE WORDS

A client I gave this book to in pre-publication form wrote me an email saying she couldn't read it—some of the stories were too re-stimulating of her own traumas. She said, "I hope in the future I will be able to read the book and not get upset. Guess I'm just too sensitive!!!!????!!!!"

I suggested that she tap (using EFT) while she was reading it, either repeatedly up and down all the points as she read, or tapping just on the karate chop point, whichever seemed to work best for her.

That turned out to be a good idea. She ended up reading the whole book, finding it very useful, and offering a list of grammar and spelling corrections! (*Thank you!*) As a result of her comments, I have placed the instructions about how to do EFT near the beginning of the book.

I recommend that you pay attention to your inner responses as you read, and take note of what specifically brings up an emotional reaction in you.

Tap while you read: at any disturbing point, actually stop *right then* and tap for anything that particularly captures your attention and makes you feel sad, upset or fearful.

Tap if you find yourself caught in a memory that re-stimulates

Profoundly light-hearted strategies for unsticking stuck stuff

feelings that you have been trying to keep buried, or thought you had left behind.

```
   v °   ° > i ° V > i ° v °   ^ i v °
    i °  ° i «  i °  ^ ° L   ] °
   ^ °  i ° ^  «  i ° > V  ° v ° i> `  } °  °
 V >  ° L i ° >  ° i>   } ° i « i  i V i ° v  °
```

DISCLAIMER

Though Emotional Freedom Techniques is still considered experimental, it has yielded exceptional results in the treatment of psychological and physical problems. It is widely used by therapists, nurses, physicians, psychiatrists, acupuncturists, and many other health care workers and other professionals, including teachers and "regular people."

EFT is not a substitute for appropriate medical care or mental health treatment. I personally have never experienced any ill effects from using EFT, but you must take full responsibility for your own well-being. Advise others to do the same. I would recommend that you begin by working with a skilled practitioner, and make sure you have resources available if you should find that you need assistance.

I am certified as a Master Practitioner of Emotional Freedom Techniques (EFT), certified as a Clinical Hypnotherapist (by AnchorPoint Associates, and registered with American Council of Hypnotist Examiners), certified as a Consultant in Energy Psychology, and certified as a Master Practitioner and Health Practitioner in Neuro-Linguistic Programming. I am a registered minister with the Universal Life Church, and a Frameworks Life Coach certified by InnerLinks Associates. I am not a Wisconsin State licensed mental health professional and I do not provide psychotherapy or other mental health services which would require a Wisconsin State license.

No guarantee is offered or implied that you will be helped by this work.

```
9   °    >   ]°  °>L    °  ° ^i°    °
>} >   ]°> '°« ^   i°    }°> i° i°
'iV ' }°v>V   ^°  °>V  i }°^ V V i^^v  °
              V  i^
```

2: I WANT TO WANT TO HEAL

As we work with the concepts in this book, you will read about many of the ways we sabotage our healing.

Our saboteurs are on the job 24/7, and, believe it or not, they are trying to make life better for us. They really are doing their very best, in a manner of speaking, to bring our attention to making sure that we take good care of ourselves.

It is useful to approach our life-healing work with the intention to transform these saboteurs into allies on our behalf, LOTS of options that lead to our feeling good instead of bad.

Silvia Hartmann has long been a creative innovator and developer in the field of Energy Psychology. Below is an article she wrote for EFT founder Gary Craig's website, EmoFree.com on doing EFT tapping in order to, in her words, "build a real and powerful motivation from the inside out for a person on a wide range of topics and really help with deep and lasting change."

Wanting to Want to Heal…

I had recently an occasion to advise a long term addict on the use of EFT to help make some inroads into a long standing and very entrenched problem.

They had previously tried all manner of opening statements and approaches in self help but nothing had budged; I just spent some time finding out what topics they had tried to cover.

These included a wide variety of significant experiences and entrainments, notably:

✳ Having a same-sex parent who had had the same addiction all their lives, including during this person's pregnancy

✳ The many failures to "beat the addiction" by the parent who still had it when they died from it

✳ Their own withdrawal traumas and failures to change their own patterns

✳ Formative experiences with the substance

✳ The person's beliefs and experiences around the entire scenario

✳ And finally, their entrenched and automatic behaviours which they suspected to be simply learned, now, and which would run even in the absence of underlying drivers.

I would add to that, further, that this person seemed to me to have a very high-level of background stress all the time; they were very anxious just as a bye-the-bye and even though the situation was as non-threatening as could be (we were simply having a discussion, with no idea suggested that the addiction would be tackled at all); they confirmed that they were indeed, always very nervous and had always been.

I asked them to pick out one of the most impactful opening statements they'd ever come across and just tap it to show me how they did it, and so I could get a sense of what was happening. It was really interesting to observe and sense; it was a good opening statement, and the person applied themselves to the task of tapping the round most earnestly, but there was really absolutely no response I could detect, no energy shift or any form of change in their voice or bearing as they went through the points.

I had the strong sense that the entire system was "locked down" (not reversed), and on an intuition, asked them to try the opening statement of, "I want to be free of this addiction."

Once again, they applied themselves earnestly but that same sense of lock-down was most apparent again; then I had a very good idea.

I asked them to tap, instead, for, "I want to want to overcome the addiction," and as though these had been the magic words, things began to happen as soon as they tapped the Karate Chop point.

The very first thing was that the person started to cry spontaneously and when they recovered use of their voice, there was tremendous longing and real emotion present for the first time. On this round, there was yawning, movement, insights and not just the energy system, but the entire person seemed to be coming to life on the topic at last.

What came out of this round was a whole list of criteria and reasons as to why the person had not ever really wanted to want to give up their addiction; as well as a number of prerequisites which had to be dealt with before they could allow themselves to really want to end this, put it in the past and start a new life.

Amongst the list were:

✻ They would have to be sure that they weren't being disrespectful or unloving to the parent by living a different life and in essence, needed the parents' approval (although deceased) to be allowed to want to end it

✻ They would have to have some hope or faith that it could be done at all in the absence of any personal or observed proof of any kind that it was possible

✻ They would have to be not as terrified of withdrawal trauma and pain as they were because they simply could not want something that hurt and frightened them that much

Profoundly light-hearted strategies for unsticking stuck stuff

THE 8 MASTER KEYS TO HEALING WHAT HURTS

Opening statements for these pre-requisites were duly found, and when they were applied, the person was very engaged and responsive, very motivated and the energy system responded also very well indeed to each round which was applied.

It was really most fascinating to observe how things were unfolding; and with hindsight, it was really quite obvious that this person had needed a bridging step into the first step to starting on changing their behaviours and their lives.

It had always been quietly presumed that of course they wanted to change this health threatening and frightening problem which had killed their parent; and the usual approach of looking for "benefits," which may have counter-balanced the away-from motivation, only produced side effects, essentially lemonade the person had made from the lemons they had been dealt.

But of course, every addictions counsellor knows that a true motivation and desire for change is just about the only thing that can get a person into true long term and lasting change; and to build up the desire to WANT TO change FIRST and to take the blockers to this out of the way is logical, effective and very motivational indeed.

This double phrasing of "I want to want to ... (change, stop doing X, stop feeling Y, stop remembering Z, etc)" is an interesting neurological event that can be used in many situations, where, although there may be logical reasons for doing or not doing something different, still a real heartfelt motivation seems to be lacking.

A different version of this could be:

"I want to be able to want to (_____)," to make it easier to understand; and investigative versions are possible also, such as:

❋ "I don't understand why I don't want to change,"

Profoundly light-hearted strategies for unsticking stuck stuff

THE 8 MASTER KEYS TO HEALING WHAT HURTS

✳ "I don't know what I would need to allow myself to want to change,"

✳ "I just can't allow myself to really want to change because..."

✳ "I wonder what else I can do to really motivate myself to want to change,"

✳ "Before I can wholeheartedly commit myself to wanting this change, I would have to..."

✳ ... and so forth, to discover what is standing in the way of a real desire to power all further endeavours; and of course, further and regular application of EFT for cravings, fears, doubts etc. as well.

I would add that this is not just a pattern to help motivate addicts towards change and unlock "frozen" systems, but that statements such as:

"I want to want to be loved"

"I want to want to be healthy"

"I want to want to be happy"

"I want to want to be wealthy"

... and so forth can be used to build *a real and powerful motivation* from the inside out for a person on a wide range of topics, and really help with deep and lasting change.

Silvia Hartmann, PhD
Starfields.org
reprinted with permission

THE 8 MASTER KEYS TO HEALING WHAT HURTS

NOTES

3: LEARN AND USE EFT

WHAT IS EFT?

EFT is a rapid, highly effective, easy-to-learn self-healing technique.

Remember this, first and foremost:

```
 °V    V °«>  °  °  i i °«  ^V > ]°
i   >  °  °i >  ° °^°>L  ° i°^     °
 i°i °  ^i i^°>L  °  °i«i iV i°
```

I teach people an easy-to-learn method of dissolving anxiety and stress, easing both physical and emotional pain, releasing fears and negative or limiting beliefs of any kind. It is based on five thousand years of practical study in Traditional Chinese Medicine about the way the energy system of the body is affected by negative emotion.

EFT works literally in a matter of minutes, replacing emotional distress with a form of peace, calm or confidence.

This remarkable and refreshing new approach is called Emotional Freedom Techniques (EFT).

In essence it is like yoga for the emotions and the spirit, or a psychological version of acupuncture except that needles aren't necessary.

EFT involves tapping gently on the stress relief points of the body with the fingertips, places we instinctively touch or rub anyway when we are upset, like around the eyes and on the chest.

Features

- ❋ The results are usually long lasting.
- ❋ The process is relatively gentle.
- ❋ Most people can apply the techniques to themselves.
- ❋ It is inexpensive to learn and use, and easy to teach in a group while still maintaining individual privacy.
- ❋ It often provides relief for physical and emotional pain, headaches and addictive cravings.

Where it has been useful

EFT has been proven clinically effective in the Veterans Administration with many of our Vietnam War Veterans. It has helped in weight-loss programs, and has also assisted students with "learning blocks."

EFT has provided noticeable gains in many performance areas such as sports, music and public speaking. Those who meditate find that EFT allows them to "go deeper" and mental health professionals are reporting dramatic improvements in their clients' well being.

For more information

EFT does not do everything for everyone and is still in the experimental stage. However, the clinical results over the last five years have been remarkable. For more information, visit Gary Craig's site at emofree.com; or go to EFTBooks.com. This is a wonderful healing tool that is easy to learn, highly effective, and an empowering self care tool that puts the ability to clear your path toward inner peace literally into your own hands.

I think it is best to get started by working with an accomplished practitioner for a time to get experience and a sense of how to use these techniques creatively for greatest effectiveness. From there, you can heal your own life.

A client recently sent this comment to me:

"EFT is astonishing both in its simplicity and its effectiveness in dislodging and removing emotional hurts and painful memories. I have found it powerful in healing present-time emotional pain (self hatred and self rejection) and in removing the hurt of events long past.

"I experienced liberation from difficult childhood experiences, and not only was the past healed, but I was empowered through the process so that my current habits of better self care were reinforced and strengthened."

The idea that, by using EFT, we can take greater responsibility for our own emotional and physical well-being is more than exciting!

On the following pages you will find a discription of how to use EFT, and illustrations of the tapping points.

THE EFT PROCESS: ﹥ ﹅ ﹥ } ﹥ ^ ° ^ ﹥ ° ° « ﹥ } i ° n fi

The set-up statement:

A. Say statements 1 - 3 in a complete set three times as you strike the Karate Chop Point:

> **1.** Even though I ____ (insert your phrase here) ____

> **2.** I deeply and completely accept myself (or, if for a child: I'm a great kid, or another appropriate phrase)

> **3.** and I choose _____ (insert your phrase here) ____

The Tapping Sequence:

B. Repeat the reminder phrase (the gist of the Even Though statement) as you tap on the face and body

C. Repeat the reminder, or "I choose" phrase as you tap down the points on the face & body

---

An example:

A. Striking the Karate Chop Point, say out loud:
> **1.** Even though I can't sleep
> **2.** I deeply and completely accept myself
> **3.** And I choose to sleep well and wake up refreshed

B. Tapping the issue:

> Repeat "can't sleep," "can't sleep," etc., as you tap on the points. Do two rounds minimum; do more if necessary

C. Tapping the choice:

> Repeat "sleep well," "awaken refreshed," "sleep well," "awaken refreshed," etc., as you tap on the points on the face and body.

Do a minimum of two rounds tapping; do more if it feels right. Add the Finger Points and/or The Gamut for stubborn issues.

❋ ❋ ❋

I have included in this book the most commonly referred to points on page 20 and 21: the Karate Chop Point and the Main Tapping Points.

For a complete tutorial how to use the Emotional Freedom Techniques, refer to the accompanying *8 Master Keys Discovery Book*. You will find detailed instructions, stories and examples how to use EFT, and illustrations of all the points.

❋ ❋ ❋

THE KARATE CHOP POINT

KARATE CHOP POINT

strike the Karate Chop Point gently with either the tips of the first two fingers or the inside of the combined flattened fingers of the other hand

Profoundly light-hearted strategies for unsticking stuck stuff

THE TAPPING SPOTS

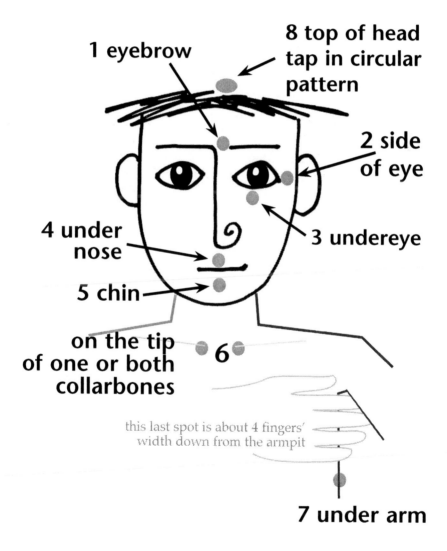

1 eyebrow

8 top of head tap in circular pattern

2 side of eye

3 undereye

4 under nose

5 chin

on the tip of one or both collarbones

6

this last spot is about 4 fingers' width down from the armpit

7 under arm

NOTES

2
HEALING FROM "SOUL ABUSE"

Chronic physical and emotional pain calls for healing at the deepest levels of identity.

EFT and other Energy Psychology techniques offer the opportunity for healing at this level.

This book is about a recipe for tapping into this well of strength and courage in us, using Emotional Freedom Techniques (EFT). The first chapter in the book will teach you how to do EFT.

This book is not about healing what hurts. It is about healing our thinking. The real theme here is healing pain by the deeper work of healing our lives.

Healing from "Soul Abuse"

One of the first questions I ask someone, after I have heard a bit about what is troubling them, is, "What do you want?"

If they stop breathing and look blank, or if they begin to talk about not even knowing what they want or about needing a sense of purpose or meaning or direction, I know I have found someone who has probably been on the receiving end of what I have come to think of as "soul abuse."

7 i ° >   ° > i ° i « i i V i ' ° " ^   ° > L ^ i » ° °

THE 8 MASTER KEYS TO HEALING WHAT HURTS

It is about people's collective inhumanity to each other: when we consciously or unconsciously threaten, shame, make over-critical comments or judgments, discount, trivialize, or act violently toward another. That is soul abuse.

Repeated soul abuse of children leads to their growing up entangled in a web of *self*-criticism and limiting beliefs about self worth and what is possible in the world.

Soul abuse can take place within/inside an individual (among internal parts), between individuals, or between groups, genders, races, nations, or species.

```
 °Li ii°  >  °  °^«    >  °   °>^°   >  ^°^°
   °  i>  °  °  °i>  °   °>L ^ i°  >   i
   °
```

Now, I have some hesitation about using the actual words "soul abuse." In a world filled with such oppression of people's lives, it is a sort of luxury to be in a position to talk about oppression of the soul. In fact, it may be that the soul cannot actually be abused. But soul abuse is a term that people understand instantly, and one that carries the spirit, so to speak, and the story of a concept that has meaning for them.

The concept of healing from soul abuse comes out of my search to find ways to frame this experience of disconnection from meaning, purpose and worth, and, in partnership with a client, to discover how to foster a renewed awareness of the connection to Source, whatever that might mean to him or her.

At some point early in my work with someone, I will tell them a kind of story or metaphor about my take on the Meaning of Life. It incorporates ideas that have been germinating, growing and reseeding in my thinking for years, and it offers a way for people (and me) to reframe suffering.

This story may or may not be true, but like any good metaphor, it offers a way of thinking about life that helps to explain things, and helps people to feel better and more hopeful and more powerful about it all. And perhaps even to feel useful in the universe.

I think that the meaning of life is always there in the story we choose to tell ourselves about it, and I always tend toward choosing a fascinating story full of positive intentions, instead of a boring, scary or depressing one.

People invariably like this story that I tell them, and feel comforted by it. So whether or not it is "true," there is truth in there somewhere. Without defining too tightly what any of this means, I begin to talk about thinking of life as a partnership between the "soul" and the "body."

The body/mind/personality, I say, has the sacred job of carrying the pattern of the human life, the positive and negative tendencies, the challenges, the learnings, and the many strengths acquired over time.

The soul carries a connection with Spirit, and a Big Picture sense of mission and purpose. It probably has its own blind spots and tendencies toward misalignment.
Anything that manifests as pain in the personality represents some pattern of unintegrated energy that the personality has agreed to hold on behalf of the evolution of consciousness, for the purpose of transformation.

In some way, I continue, the soul and the body/mind/personality choose to partner for the purpose of figuring out together how to transform, integrate, and align the un-integrated, mis-aligned and dis-ordered energy in the universe that the personality carries.

In this context, each human life is a scene in a larger tapestry, a universal story about the outworking of limiting beliefs.
These limiting energy patterns have been passed down through many generations of a family as its members weave their various strands together over time, each generation doing its bit to shine up the picture as best it can.

Now, body and soul forget all this as they actually enter a life together. The personality experiences the dissonance as suffering. It learns over time how to dissociate—to push the pain away, ignore it, "stuff it," in order to survive. (This causes lots of problems later on.) As the soul becomes aware of the magnitude of what it has taken on to do, it may feel overwhelmed.   One part or another may begin to find ways to sabotage the partnership.

So, as I continue to tell my client this story, I add the idea that each of us is given, and chooses, a corner of the universe of which to be the custodian: to clean and shine it up, to take good care of it. When we become aware of it, our corner may be pretty dark and grungy, loud and disjointed, scary and unsafe. Like a baby covered in poop, the beauty and perfection may not be readily apparent, but it *is* there.

```
  °vii °  > ° °^°    ° L]° i >  ° i« « ^i°
 v°   ° i^]° ° ^V i ° > ' ° > ^v   ° > i i °
  ' ^v } i^°   °   iV  i ° v° i°        '
```

And then I say, "Good for you, because the fact that you are here means that you are choosing in this life to do your best to end that old pattern of soul abuse that had been passed along in your heritage for so many generations.

"Isn't it good to know that this suffering and negativity and pain is not about *you*?"

Your life is a purpose and a mission and a work that you have chosen to do as a gift to the evolution of consciousness in the universe. This means that you will have lots of help, from seen and unseen sources, because the universe deeply supports this process. The universe is *about* this process.

Doing this work together is soul work. It is healing. The healing of any of us helps the healing of all of us. So let's get started!

❋ ❋ ❋ ❋ ❋

3
A STORY OF HURTING AND HEALING

"Pushing *through* fear is less frightening than living with the underlying fear that comes from a feeling of helplessness."

Susan Jeffers

We love the miracles that abound in so many stories of people using EFT, and it is important to remember that this is always possible! At the same time, it doesn't always work that way. We are not just broken machines needing to be fixed. Often the journey itself is the healing.

Sometimes healing pain through the deeper work of healing our lives may feel too difficult, or too much to ask in the current situation.

People who are Sensitive Idealists often have the inner program that says: "I have to tough this out. I just have to get through it. I have to soldier on. I can do this. No one is going to help me. I shouldn't ask for help anyway."

SALLY

Here is a journey story about how this transformative process can look in an actual life, the story of one sensitive woman's on-going healing journey with EFT. **It contains many of the themes that will show up throughout this book.**

Now, Sally's process of healing into her Wealth-Being is not tidily arranged in one-minute wonders. It is a bumpy road, like the one we are all on, and it continues today. She didn't heal and then live happily ever after. She is learning to live happily, now, and *therefore* ever after.

Initially, I had two in-person EFT sessions with Sally, who was experiencing serious chronic physical and emotional pain. She stopped coming after these two sessions, and I believe it was because she was feeling overwhelmed. It was becoming apparent that she was going to have to make some deep life changes, and that was feeling scary to her. She did resume our sessions several months later.

Here is how our work together evolved:

It began with an email to me from Sally. We have had many sessions together by now, mostly by telephone. She is a very bright and articulate woman. Early on, I realized that the dialogue we were establishing by email between sessions could serve as a valuable resource for other people, so I saved them. I have included a sampling here so you can get a sense of how a person's creative use of EFT can create profound shifts. I have changed her name, edited out her personal references, and include all of her words with her permission.

A dream come true....

I was so thrilled to find your website on the Internet. For the first time since my chronic back pain started 16 years ago, I am (geographically) close enough to take advantage of treatment from someone who is an advocate of John Sarno's methods. I am anxious to tell you a little about myself and to find out if indeed I could benefit from what you and Dr. Selfridge have to offer.

THE 8 MASTER KEYS TO HEALING WHAT HURTS

I am a 58 year-old married woman with no children. Sixteen years ago I developed severe, debilitating low back, buttock, and left leg pain. I had every test imaginable, CT scans, MRI imaging, and a myelogram. All test results were negative. This sent me into a nosedive of depression and I ended up with a psychiatrist who gave me anti-depressives, anti-anxiety medication and little more. I also went through a pain clinic. That did me no good. I tried Chinese medicine, including acupuncture and herbal remedies. That did not help in any measurable way.

My condition would get a little better, I'd attempt to do a little more and boom, I'd find myself right back where I started from. I had to quit my job and was fortunate to be able to get Social Security Disability, which I am still on. All of this caused a great deal of strain in my marriage and nearly broke it up. But we persevered and we still love each other very much. But that is not to say that we wouldn't be even happier if I found a cure for my back pain!

About 1995 or so I was given Dr. Sarno's book "Healing Back Pain." I devoured it. It seemed like a dream come true. But I was not able to "cure" myself with it as some people have, and I was too far away to be a patient of his, so I did what I could and that was search for a psychotherapist who did "in depth" work. The first one I went to did not work out. It was not until I found (a good psychologist) in early 1999 that we really started working.

By that time I had gotten Sarno's "The MindBody Prescription," and I saw myself immediately in it. I remembered things I had repressed from childhood such as how physically abusive my father was to my mother, and how emotionally abusive he was to both of us. I got very mixed messages in childhood about how on the one hand women were never as good as men, and yet there were high expectations put on me as an only child. I worked with (the psychologist) until 2003 when we moved (to another area).

By this time, my pain had started to ease up and I was able to tolerate more physical activity. However, the physical activity came too late to prevent me from getting osteoporosis and suffering a broken

Profoundly light-hearted strategies for unsticking stuck stuff

hip about a year ago. The beginning of the pain coincided with a premature menopause, and osteoporosis was the result. I am now being treated aggressively for that.

I guess the real reason I started searching now for a "Sarno" alternative, is what has been in the news about NSAIDS. I have been taking them most of the last 16 years, and I'm now worried about the consequences of my continuing them. Also, my life has calmed down some. We moved partly for my husband's business and also to care for my aging father who had developed dementia. After a horrible few years seeing to his needs, he finally passed away about a year ago, and I'm starting to feel it is time for me to focus on myself.

 All this brings me to you and your program. I would love to hear from you as soon as possible, by mail, e-mail, or phone. My greatest problem is my fear of the pain. It overshadows my whole life and I would love to find a way to deal with it.

Sally came for her first session, driving across the state with her husband, an uncomfortable trip for her.

I asked when the pain in her back had started, and what was going on then in her life. She smiled wryly and said, "It was 1989 and my life was a mess."

She went on to describe herself as "career impaired," saying that she couldn't find a career that was good for her - everything she did left her feeling stressed, overwhelmed and like she had failed. Because she was detail oriented and sensitive to people, she always found herself in pressured management positions. Eventually she would be overtaken by stress, unable to relax, on edge, always feeling like there was something she should be doing. No matter how much she did, Sally felt she was not doing enough.

"There wasn't any particular event," she said, "that triggered my

Profoundly light-hearted strategies for unsticking stuck stuff

back pain, unless it was over-stretching at a yoga class. Right at the same time I had some new shoes that were hard on my feet. And then I was sitting in a restaurant, and my back started hurting. The pain just continued to get worse."

Sally entered what would become years of seeing doctor after doctor, receiving treatment after treatment from medical practitioners. She had a CT scan, an EMG, an MRI. She saw a neurosurgeon. She had a myelogram and a spinal tap. She took muscle relaxants and NSAIDs. She saw an osteopath. She saw a psychiatrist who told her she had a "fine childhood," and that she "didn't need psychotherapy."

Sally came across Dr. John Sarno's books (*Healing Back Pain: The Mind Body Connection; The Mind Body Prescription: Healing the Body, Healing the Pain; Mind Over Back Pain*), and read there repeatedly that back pain is the body's response to repressed emotion stemming from childhood memories.

That led her into four years of therapy ("it did help some") during which she "worked through many issues around my father from my childhood."

During these years her father divorced her mother, her husband lost his job, she developed osteoporosis, and then her hip broke ("I didn't break my hip, it just broke."). And then her father died.

The pain was getting worse...

I asked Sally to describe her pain to me. "It is pain in my left buttock, mostly," she said, "sometimes going down my leg. It hurts mostly when I'm sitting."

I always want a description that goes deeper than the facts, one that carries more information.

I asked her to create a metaphor of the pain – what does it feel like? "It feels like something is gripping onto my left buttock," she said, "clinching tighter and tighter. Like a big pincer. The pain feels red, intense." She rated the pain in her buttock at an 8 out of a possible 10, with 10 being the worst.

We did some tapping for "this gripping pain in my left buttock…this clinching pincer in my left buttock…this red, intense pain in my left buttock…"

I asked what emotions were connected to this pain.

She talked about grief and anger, the life she was losing, all the things she could no longer do. We tapped for the emotions.

All of this tapping helped a little, but when I asked what it felt like now, she really got on a roll. "It is like a malicious little leprechaun with a tiny set of needles. He is sticking me and sticking me! He is saying, 'See - I'm still here! You can't get rid of me!'"

When I asked what her self-talk was about this pain, her response was instant: "Oh why did this happen to me? Why am I being punished??"

We asked the leprechaun.

"So Sally," I said. "Imagine that you can ask this leprechaun a question. Ask him what he is trying to get FOR you through these needles and this pain?" She thought a minute, and then said, "He is just trying to get a rise out of me!"

Sensing some intuitive correspondences lining up in my head, I began by asking, "What has been a pain in the ass for you?"

"My father, she replied promptly."
And this: "Sally, what have you been sitting on?"

"Hmmm…" she paused. "My past."

"Go deeper," I said. "What, deep in you, have you been sitting on, all your life?"

Profoundly light-hearted strategies for unsticking stuck stuff

"My self-confidence," she answered, taking a deep breath. "My faith in myself."

I wanted to know what she would be doing if she *had* confidence and faith in herself.

She thought a minute and said, "I would work in a library, drive, re-establish a sexual relationship with my husband, stop worrying about so many things, see the good side of things instead of the bad. I would love myself more. I would come out of the light from the darkness. I would get off some of the drugs I am on. I would be out in the world more. I would have fewer self-defeating thoughts, more life-affirming thoughts. I would have serenity."

"So!" I offered, "the leprechaun has for all this time been trying to get your attention through all this pain to *get a rise* out of you! He wants you to rise up from your past, get up off your butt, rise to your own serenity. He wants you to sit in serenity!"

Sally looked surprised and smiled. She thought for some long moments, her eyes filling with tears. I sat quietly, giving her space to process these revelations.

"You know," she said, "for the first time, after all these years, I feel like I have a chance."

"I *have* been sitting on my past, rather than in my serenity. I feel like today has lifted me from the self-involved world I have lived in…like the trees that grow so tall…toward the sun rather than away from it.

This gives me hope, hope with wings." (I liked that, "hope with wings.")

I smiled at her. "It has all been sitting there, waiting to arise in you," I said.

I talked for a bit about her words "self-involved," about how I think of self as being capitalized: Self.

To me, Self means the soul, what is deepest and best and strongest, what is most creative and most loving and kind and passionate and purposeful.

As well as all the rest of us too, all the parts of us that mean well but so often wander astray. So those words "self-ish," "self-involved," "self-centered," actually mean CARE FOR THE SOUL, care for myself.

```
ˋ°  v ° i° ˋ ‰  °V > i°v  °    °    °^   ^]°    °
         °^i i^]°      °              ¶
```

I got a flash of an image of one of those old fashioned dolls that can be turned upside down so the skirt falls down over its head to reveal another head and torso and outfit, another whole doll being.

You can flip them back and forth, two beings in one. Self-involved/soul-involved. It is all the same thing.

"All of **who you most deeply are** has always been **sitting there**, waiting to **stand up for yourself** and come out…" (I delivered this brief message to her unconscious mind, reframing the theme of sitting that had threaded through our time together that day….).

I could see skepticism still remaining in her face as we talked and tapped together, working with the phrases she had used, her emotions of grief and anger, ("Why did this happen to me? Why am I being punished?").

But she responded very well to EFT. The pain diminished significantly.

As we made our next appointment, I thought of what I wanted to ask her the next time she came: I would preface our session with a brief review of her long history with pain, paralleled with her long history of urgently seeking healing from pain. With such strong intention to find relief, why has healing been so elusive? What has held pain in place? I would ask her to imagine *actually healing,* and what that might be like.

And then a seemingly strange, but very powerful question came to me:

What might be uncomfortable about healing? What might you lose?

I gave Sally the tapping instructions to take home and practice with her symptoms. She left with tears in her eyes.

❋ ❋ ❋

A war zone within

A few days later I got this email from her: I didn't think I'd have to contact you this soon. I left on Wednesday feeling like we had had an excellent session. The problems started when I got back home again.

I feel like my whole self is a war zone. The fight is between wanting to desperately hang on to the "old" way of living that I am so used to, and just as desperately wanting to change to a "new" way of living without the pain. I can't stop thinking about the pain. I faithfully do the tapping exercises and they do work to calm me, and help to relieve the pain, but soon the cycle of worry and fretting and pain starts up again. I wake up every morning in a near panic. Actually, this morning I did the tapping in bed before I ever got up, and it did help some.

Can you offer any suggestions or comments? Does this happen to other people? *Does it ever go away?*

It's a good sign!

Thank you, Sally, for your email. I think that what you are experiencing is normal, and actually a very good sign, even though it doesn't feel so good.

It means that the "parts" of you (like that leprechaun) that are in control of your pain are realizing that you are changing your internal balance, and taking charge in a way that you perhaps haven't before.

‰ ^° i°ii L '° ^ 'i° ^°^> }]°" }'°
}^°> i°V > } }° °ii°> '°i°' ‰ °
° °i°> i°> it»

The part of you that is in control of the pain has had, believe it or not, a positive purpose in your life, and that part of you will suffer a lot in order for that purpose to be carried out. In some way we don't understand yet, pain is the tool as well. But understanding all that is the job of our next session!

So I am not surprised that you are having some trouble. In addition to continuing to tap for the pain as you have been, I suggest that you take the phrases from your email that I have isolated for you below, and tap for them as well. Insert them into the "problem space" and do the tapping as usual.

Even though:

- I didn't think I'd have to contact Rue this soon...
- I left on Wednesday feeling like we had had an excellent session...
- The problems started when I got back home again...
- I feel like my whole self is a war zone...
- The fight is between wanting to desperately hang on to the "old" way of living that I am so used to...

❋ I am just as desperately wanting to change to a "new" way of living without the pain...

❋ I can't stop thinking about the pain...

❋ I faithfully do the tapping exercises...

❋ ...they do work to calm me, and help to relieve the pain, but soon the cycle of worry and fretting and pain starts up again...

❋ I wake up every morning in a near panic...

This does, indeed, happen to other people! And it does go away. The fact that you are getting relief from your own tapping is a very good indication. Let me know how it goes.

More questions from Sally:

Thank you so much for responding so quickly to my email. It gave me a tremendous boost. Since then, the "war" has quieted down. In fact, I feel calmer than I have felt in a long time. I don't know if this will last, of course. I can't believe the power that controls my pain is going to give up that quickly!

I have another question: Since I have had this pain for so long, I have developed strategies for dealing with it. For example, never sitting in certain chairs for very long, using a recliner when watching television, etc. In other words, circumventing the pain.

So, for the last few days I have not had much pain because I have been doing all these things. Should I be doing this? Should I be consciously trying to face the pain head-on by sitting too long in the wrong kind of chair, etc.? I get a shudder of fear at the thought of doing this, but if it is something I should be doing, I will give it my best shot. As always, I welcome your comments and suggestions.

Never force it!:

No, I would never recommend forcing a response to ANYTHING that gives you a shudder of fear.

"Giving it your best shot," "soldiering on," "I can take it if I have to,"—these are all the kinds of statements that got you where you are to begin with!

On the other hand, you *could* tap for the fear, and tap for the discomfort. You could even sit across the room and look at "the wrong kind of chair," and tap for the sensations you would expect to feel sitting in it.

Again, go through your own email wording below and separate out the individual statements and tap for them.
That in general is a good strategy. Write out all the things you think or feel about a situation, and then tap for each one (as you feel like it, of course, never because you must or should, or because you can take it!). So glad you are finding some calm. Good sign of what is to come!

A second session

Sally came for a second session that went deeply into the emotional base of the pain.

Once again, EFT worked well to reduce the pain. However, this time, *when the intensity went down in one area of her body the pain began to move around to other areas.* That was disconcerting to her, but seemed like a good sign to me that things were moving inside.

I had asked her, "If the pain had a positive intention, what is it doing for you?" She answered that it protected her from having to deal with all the issues in her life. She just wanted to be taken care of.

I took the opportunity now to ask if there was a downside to healing. What would be uncomfortable about healing?

What would you lose?

She said, "The downside would be all the complications. I would have to go off my $800 Social Security Disability payments. I would have to face my job dilemma. I'd have to face sexuality again. I would lose the way I am now living. I would lose what I know about how to live. I would have to learn to do life all over again.

"I would have to face the question, 'Who am I?' I would have to explore what is my real relationship with my husband, friends, family. I would have to spend more time with people, with my extended family. I am a shy person - that would be overwhelming."

She was in tears now. "I am so confused. I want the pain to go away and I am afraid that it won't. But it would be such a big change if it did. I don't deal with change very well. It is a big big job!"

Sally talked more about her fear of change:
"I am not able to deal with change.
I have a fear that something bad will happen if I make changes.
I feel a tensing up in my behind, my sit muscles, cramping as if the muscles are being squeezed.
I can't do this.
I don't know how.
I am a perfectionist.
What if I made a mistake? That would mean I wasn't perfect and *I am supposed to be perfect.*"

This last comment led to a discussion of her childhood. It turned out that her mother had not wanted to have any children, but when her father came home from the war he *did* want for them to have children.

Her parents had almost come to a divorce over this disagreement. Her mother finally agreed to have one child. But this deep disagreement was never talked about in the family after Sally was born. She only learned of how she came to be born after her mother died. Virtually the first thing her father said to her after her mother's death was "You know, your mother never wanted to have any children."

Sally grew up with the belief that,
"I have to be perfect in order to live."

We tapped on all of this. Each of her comments about fear of change was an excellent set-up statement.

We made another appointment. Even though it was becoming clear to her that healing the pain was going to require her to consider making major changes in her life, and she was still somewhat fearful, Sally left, again feeling hopeful.

Cancellation

Then I got this email from her: I am writing to cancel our appointment next Tuesday. As much as I appreciate all your efforts, I am finding that trying to face up to my "pain producer" is proving too difficult. I spent the last two days in misery, both physically and psychologically.

The tapping worked, but only temporarily. Yesterday, the pain expanded to both my legs and I could hardly walk. The tapping was unsuccessful in dealing with it.
I can only hope that the time will come when I feel I can do this kind of work. I am so very sorry I have to do this. It looked like such a promising course of action to take.

If you have any feedback for me, I'd appreciate hearing it. I enjoyed working with you and wish you much success in the future.

I support you!

I wrote back: I am so sorry to hear that you have been so miserable. And also sorry that you want to cancel our appointment.

While I totally respect your decision, and I absolutely support you to do what is best for you, still I want to invite you to try out another idea.

Remember in our last session when the pain began to move around after we had some successes in reducing it? It is possible that the severity of your current reaction is actually yet another indication that our approach is working, but that we have possibly gone too fast and done "too well."

You are bright and responsive and intuitive, and you caught on to this new approach really quickly. I am thinking that maybe the part of you that has been running this pain strategy needs for us to back off.

Perhaps, somewhere inside and maybe even unconsciously, you may be feeling some significant fear that the work we have begun will strip you of some of the defenses in your life and leave you exposed and vulnerable to old challenges.

So the part of you that has been protecting you in an odd way through your pain, is continuing to do that by giving you even more pain to make sure that you keep the status quo in place.

That part of you means well, and in some ways it has been useful in the past, but it is using an old, very limited strategy that for a long time now has been hurting more than it is helping. There is now another part of you that deeply wants to heal from the pain - and it has recently become more hopeful, which is upsetting the balance, the ecology that you had created inside.

These two parts of you are in conflict. Right now the pain producer is still in charge, and probably is feeling threatened by the hopeful part.

Profoundly light-hearted strategies for unsticking stuck stuff

THE 8 MASTER KEYS TO HEALING WHAT HURTS

But still, I believe that leprechaun pain producer has a positive purpose for you in your life, even though that may sound odd and not be evident on the face of things.

I am wondering if we might approach the "pain producer" more slowly and gently, first acknowledging its usefulness in your life, and the reasons for its resistance.

Eventually, in a timing that is comfortable for you/it, we can invite it to become an ally on your path toward health instead of treating it as the "enemy."

Together we could (and/or you could try this on your own too) tap using phrases like:

Even though...
❋ I am not ready to do this work...
❋ this is too overwhelming...
❋ I am getting worse instead of better...
❋ this is not working...
❋ I really don't want to do this...
❋ facing up to my pain producer is too difficult...
❋ I appreciate Rue's efforts...
❋ I enjoy working with Rue...
❋ I spent the last two days in misery, both physically and psychologically...
❋ the tapping worked, but only temporarily...
❋ the pain expanded to both my legs and I could hardly walk....
❋ the tapping was unsuccessful in dealing with the pain...
❋ I hope the time will come when I feel I can do this kind of work...

❈ it looked like such a promising course of action to take...

❈ I am so very sorry I have to do this....

❈ I am not ready for this but I do wish Rue success with other people...

We would keep using phrases like this until the pain producer part no longer feels attacked, and is more willing to explore new, better, more effective ways of getting what it has been trying to get for you all these years. It *is* kind of an irresistible proposition for such a powerful part as this pain producer is.
We want it to know that we are on its side, in the sense that it has been doing its limited best to make your life bearable, even livable.

It is like a horse with blinders on – it doggedly goes on straight ahead, doing what it always has done in dutiful service to you (it thinks), not realizing that now it causes way more trouble than help. You may have heard the old adage: "If you always do what you have always done, you will always get what you have always gotten..." So these are my thoughts.

```
9   ° ` ° `i^i i°  °L i°v ii° v°« >  ]°> `°  °`°
    `i^i i° ° > i°V > }i°v°   °  ° vi°°
```

Because you have responded so well to EFT, that lets me know that you are capable of doing this, when you are ready.

On the other hand, I will respect your decision if you find that this challenge is asking too much of you at this time. In any case, I offer my abundant love and blessings -

Will she come back?

A few days later I received this note from Sally:

Dear Rue, Thank you for responding. The pain has decreased and I am starting to feel better. I have carefully read your response and I think that you may well be correct in your assessment. I certainly hope so.

My problem at the moment is that I have a family reunion coming up for which I am largely responsible. I have done a lot of work on it already, and quite a bit remains to do. I do not want to jeopardize my participation in this event and for that reason I do not think I want to do any more formal work on the chronic pain until after the event. What I may do in between now and then, I am not sure, but you have given me a lot of suggestions.

So I would like to leave it at that for now. I will get in touch with you when I am ready to resume formal work. Thank you very much for your concern and good wishes.

At this point I didn't know if she would come back. I hoped she would. There is a bright, sensitive, capable being in her that deserves to be freed from its confinement.

A few months later, as I was writing this book, I sent an email to Sally asking if I could use her words in it: "The exchange of emails that you and I had a few months ago was so interesting and such an articulate and compelling description of what a person with chronic pain suffers, that I have saved it. I am wondering if you would consent to my using it in the book, with all the references that would identify you, specifically, removed."

Sally wrote back right away, giving me permission to use her words, and adding this message:

I have spent a miserable summer, in a good deal more pain than I was in before I started seeing you. I came away from our experience with a great deal of fear and that fear seems to have pervaded my entire life.

In August after the reunion (which was a great success) I decided I was not ready to go back to EFT because of the fear. But my life seems to be spiraling downward and out of control. I think that I started something with EFT that I simply must face instead of burying my head in the sand and trying to ignore it.

> Even though I am still afraid, I think it is in my
> best interests to continue with the EFT.

I read something in Susan Jeffers' book "*Feel the Fear and Do It Anyway*" that seems to sum it up: "Pushing through fear is less frightening than living with the underlying fear that comes from a feeling of helplessness."

And I do feel helpless!

I am going to start with the suggestions you gave in your last email and I plan to be contacting you soon to start some formal work."

We did begin to work together again, by phone this time, and continued our email conversation.

It didn't take long for revelations of various kinds to appear. She recounts: The panic and terror started last night. Really bad, heart pounding, sweating, butterflies in the stomach, etc. John managed to get me calmed down and I did sleep until 5 AM, when it started up all over again. It is a nameless sort of terror.

I have been assuming it is the pain producer. And I have been tapping "Even though I am afraid of my pain producer." The pain is up, too. I have also been having terrible thoughts, like I am going to die.

I know that all of this is to be expected. Although the last time I don't remember thoughts of death. I will just keep tapping and wait for this to pass. Any encouraging words you might have would be most appreciated.

Sally - If the panic and terror come back, don't bother with the set-up statements, just tap actively up and down the points while you are feeling the emotions and physical sensations, until they quiet. Let me know how that goes. Sending you lots of love and support –

Rue, Thanks for the suggestion. I haven't had the bad panic come back, but I used the tapping alone on some grief I was feeling and it helped. I am still having a lot of trouble with anxiety. I wake up with it every morning and tap and it gets somewhat better, but then pretty quickly it returns. It seems centered in my chest and abdomen.

I responded: Here is an "assignment" for you:

❋ Make a list of all the reasons that you might not want to change/feel better/heal.

Notice what you would *lose* if you heal. What would be *uncomfortable*?

What might be some "hidden benefits" of feeling stuck/in pain/sad/in fear/in panic/etc?

❋ Imagine other better more effective ways of getting what you would lose.

❋ Imagine better ways to be comfortable, or be taken care of, or better yet, ways to make sure you get healthy doses of joy and delight into your life.

Or other ways of getting whatever this part of you that has been running the emotions and behaviors that you don't like wants *for* you. **It hasn't had any other strategies to work with besides the pain, until now.**

❉ Write those new strategies down on the page opposite to the loss/discomfort ones.

Just keep this as a running list, a kind of discussion with yourself. You don't have to do anything about the things you write—don't want to scare the pain producer. Just engage your creative mind, inviting it to consider other possibilities.

Tap on anything that looks interesting.

And then I got this from her!

I have had the most amazing thing happen while I was working on the assignment you just sent me. I was thinking about it and about all the anxiety I have been having and all of a sudden I saw a vision of a terrified little girl-little Sally—running through me desperately seeking love and attention and all those things children need, and her not finding them.

The thought also occurred to me that she might be the pain producer or part of it.

I started tapping "I love you, little Sally."

What else can I do? Also, I never asked you if positive tapping is different at all from negative tapping, e.g., "I love you" vs. "I have anxiety."

Profoundly light-hearted strategies for unsticking stuck stuff

How wonderful! Thank you so much for sharing this. I believe that this vision was sent to you as a healing opportunity.

If you think about it, all the care and attention and protection that little Sally needs can be provided, after a fashion, when *your* focus is on your pain and panic.

Using your pain, you find ways of getting taken care of, feeling safe…sort of. What you have been feeling is her fear, her emotional pain, locked in the past. She is asking you directly now to find ways of helping her to free and heal herself.

What would you do if a terrified little girl came to you for help? If that happened to me, I would gather her into my arms and hold her and rock her and tell her I would take care of her and love her to the best of my ability.

I would ask her what she feared, and what she needed, and I would do my best to take care of those needs in a healthy safe way.

I would tell her how beautiful she was, and how good, and how valuable, and how much she is loved.

I would sing to her. I would play with her. I would let her know that I was her grown up self, and that she had grown up, and was safe now.

She is frozen in the past - she does not know that she grows up to be a strong competent smart woman.

She is frozen in her fear and desperation.

Little Sally needs to know that, in growing up, she **did** learn how to find what she needed in the world.

I would tell her how smart she was to do that. But that she/I/we need now some new, better, more effective and powerful ways. The old ones that worked in the past aren't working so well any more.

I would tell her that those people in her life as a child hurt her only because they didn't know any better.

It wasn't because she was a bad girl, or not good enough. I would tell her that those grownups had been hurt in the same ways. Acting that way was all they knew, because some part of them had been frozen in the past too. They had had to leave a lot of their love behind, and so when they grew up they didn't know any more how to use it.

I would tell her that she could leave it to me, she didn't have to be afraid any more.

And I would invite her to grow up now, to become my current age, so she could make use of my knowledge of the world. I would ask her to return to me the gifts of my bright spirit, my love and joy and creativity and imagination and power that she has been carrying all these years, frozen there in fear in the past.

I would thank her.

I would promise her that I would always take care of her now.

I would do all this in my imagination, holding and rocking her, tapping on myself as I talked, just continuously tapping, and imagining that I was tapping on her. Try that...

A message from little Sally

Some weeks later, I heard from Sally again: First of all I have a message for you from little Sally. She mostly communicates with me by holding up a sign with her message on it. Yesterday she held up a sign that said, "I love Rue." And I second the emotion!

My question has to do with tapping for pain. For example, if I did have a problem with my hip implant which was causing the pain I am feeling in my left thigh, would it be possible for tapping to work to eliminate it? I am unclear about the use of EFT with pain coming from an organic cause as opposed to pain of a psychogenic nature.

First, I thank little Sally, and my sign says the same thing about her! AND, the sign I hold up for her is also a Magic Mirror—when she looks into it she can see who she really is! How beautiful, how smart, how creative, how loving, how fun...and...and...and...

Do physical pain tapping just like you would do psychogenic pain. In fact it is good and interesting to intermix the two. Imagine that your hip can talk, and ask it what it thinks about this implant, and how it feels. Tap for what ever comes up. You can even just tap up and down the points while you are having the conversation with your hip.

Also imagine that the implant can talk - what would it say about why it is there?

Imagine they are actors in a play! Create a scene with your hip, the implant, your body, and say, your healing angel. Get everyone on the same team.

Make tapping sequences for all the characters' lines in the script you come up with!

What happens to Little Sally if I heal?

I've come down a bit, in spirit, since yesterday. I think it is because I have started to think about all the "might have been's" concerning my dad, and feeling such sadness. "If only he'd been a better father to me," etc.

On another note: little Sally. I know that she needs to grow up. If she does what happens to "little Sally" who is about 5 years old? I feel like a mother who doesn't want her little girl to grow up because she is so adorable right now. Why can't she stay this way forever?

So, do I end up with a series of little Sallies, or as she grows up do all the previous Sallies disappear? (I think I would really like to skip the little Sally who is a teenager!!).

This is not surprising - don't be alarmed. These statements are perfect for tapping. Write out as many "might have beens" as you can think of. Really extend your imagination - see if you can come up with ones that "someone else" might think of, even if it doesn't feel true for you personally.

Then tap on all of them, one by one. Or you can save them for our appointment. As for your question about lovely little Sally: If you could design the perfect answer, for *you*, to this question, what would it be?

Little Sally is changing

Sally wrote: In your email you said, "If you could design the perfect answer for YOU, to this question, what would it be?"

My answer was: I would want a little Sally who could be childlike and stay the way she appears to me and ALSO have the wisdom and experience of an older Sally.

I think my answer is beginning to come true. This morning when I was vacillating about physical therapy, I asked little Sally what I should do. She very calmly held up a sign that said, "Don't go to therapy. Then later in the shower I got very upset about the pain and the therapy and my doctor, and my thoughts went to Sally, and I told her I was sorry to be so upset, and she was not upset at all. She told me that "It's OK. You are a good person. It will be all right."

 I thanked her and told her that she was one heck of a girl. Little Sally is changing, or perhaps I should say that my relationship with her is changing. I don't feel the over-whelming need to have her as a little girl.

And I am starting to get verbal messages in a voice not unlike my own. This is taking a little getting used to, but I do know that the voice is the best, most wonderful part of me. That's a really great Christmas present. I > changing!

❋ ❋ ❋ ❋ ❋

Sally is a bright, sensitive, capable being who is deeply seeking to be free from her limiting beliefs and behaviors. And at the same time she has lots of saboteur-ish parts inside that are holding on to the status quo, fearful of change.

The main thing is that her movement is definitely forward. She continues to re-point herself in the direction that she wants to go in. That is all that is asked of any of us!

```
     °L i  i i°  >  °>  °  i°   °v °V    V °« >        °
     V  ‘   ^ °  ^ °>  °   i^^ °v °  i°^   ]°
        >  °   i^^ °v °  i° ‘i             °  °

    /  ^ °   ‘ °  v °  « >   °^ °>i^^i }i    ]°
  >  °  ‘V >    °   >  °  i°« i^  ‰  ^°  i  °  vi°ii}  °
            ^°L i  }°L  V  i‘
```

The themes of chronic pain are:

❋ A sensitive temperament

❋ High intelligence and competence, even though in some ways the personal style may be disorganized

❋ A profound idealism: a deep commitment to do and be goodness in the world

❋ Painful life experiences that have lead to:
Deeply limiting beliefs abut one's worth and deserving
Willingness to put oneself "last on the list" (if on the list at all!)
Feeling overwhelmed
The feeling that, "I have to tough it out, I must get through this, I can handle it"

❋ Strong emotions: sadness, anger, fear that couldn't/can't be openly expressed

❋ Years of repressing these emotions

❋ A family/generational history of repressing emotions and disconnecting from the body

❋ Pain in the mind, body and spirit that defies medical diagnosis

Chronic physical and emotional pain calls for healing at the deepest levels of identity. EFT and other Energy Psychology techniques offer the opportunity for healing at this level.

❋ ❋ ❋ ❋ ❋

NOTES

4
THE
8 MASTER KEYS
FOR HEALING WHAT HURTS

FREE YOUR S.P.I.R.I.T.E.D. SELF!

Here is the recipe that we will use. It is a recipe for gathering information that you can use for yourself or your clients.

* Take an issue in your life, and answer each of the eight questions in this chapter about it.

* Gather all the answers to each question, and create tapping routines.

* Do a little or a lot each day.

You can't OD on EFT. (Make sure you have a life though!) You can't do this wrong. It *is* helpful to work with a practitioner, but there is a lot that you can do on your own.

I call the deepest, most powerful truth about us: "Wealth-Being."

Profoundly light-hearted strategies for unsticking stuck stuff

Wealth: The origin of the word means: Well-being, prosperity, happiness, wellness.

It is a very old word. It appears in language before 900 AD.

We think of having wealth. We wish we had more of it. It always seems elusive. "They" get to "have" wealth, not little old me.

What could it mean to BE wealth??

Where in your life are you wealthy (wealthy=well, happy, prosperous)?

Where are you poor?

```
        ° «  i  ° ^ °   i° i^      °
     v °V > }  }°i°  > °      ^«       ° °
```

Poverty is not just economic. Pain, depression, anxiety, fear, shame, worry, anger – all of this is poverty.

```
     ° ` `° i°}i°    °  i°V > }i° v °
        « i °        }¶ °°
           i i° i^  \°°
     °`° i°}i°  ^i i^° ¶ °°
 "  ° i>  }°^° °   °> `^]°  °  /
```

WITH THE 8 MASTER KEYS TO HEALING WHAT HURTS AND CREATING WEALTH-BEING!

S – Tap to reframe your **Sensitivity**
Have you ever been told, "Oh, you are just too sensitive!" ?
First, let's learn what is profoundly good about being sensitive.

P – Tap away effects of **Pain**-ful experiences from the past.
Life, especially your childhood, led you to believe that:
You don't deserve to get what you want.
It is not safe to be visible or heard.

I – Tap to reframe the limited **Identity** you took on as a result
(beliefs):
There is something wrong with me. It was my fault.
My needs aren't important.
I have to save the world   so that…/before… I can be safe.

R – Tap away the **Responses** in your body to this limited
identity (caged spirit)
You couldn't express what you really felt, so you swallowed it, and
now it is expressing as:
pain in your body
chronic illness
sabotaging behavior, like avoidance, addictions, procrastination

I – Tap the deeper positive **Intention** of the symptoms and
emotions
But deep inside you that anger or pain is really a message to you,
wanting you to know that:
I can stand up for myself, express my own truth, ask for what I want.
I deserve to take care of myself without feeling guilty!
It is safe to be visible and be heard.

Profoundly light-hearted strategies for unsticking stuck stuff

T – Tap for knowing that the **Truth** about me is...I was born good!
(and, surprise, your goodness has always been there!)
The Truth about you is that your Wealth-Being is good for the world!
I belong here. I am called to be here; I have a purpose here.
I deserve to prosper!
My truth has always been in everything I have done.

E - Evidence that you have always been this truth
Find the examples of it in your life

D - Set your **Direction**
Understand Your Yum and Yuck
Learn how to know What is Right for You
I deserve to take care of myself without feeling guilty!
Tap into your own guidance.

SELF - Be Self - ish!
It is safe to be visible and be heard
I am worthy of growing both spiritually and materially.
Tap to feed your own soul. If you don't, no one will.

❊ ❊ ❊

```
    7 i°> i°>  °  °  ^°}i i      °°
  / i° i>   }° >  °  °>V V  «  ^ °
        L i iv  ^°>  °v° ^t

      ii°9  °  > }i'°-«    t
  /> «°  °9  °  7 i>    i }   t
```

❊ ❊ ❊

S.P.I.R.I.T.E.D. SELF!

I created the mnemonic of **S.P.I.R.I.T.E.D. SELF** so you could remember the 8 questions more easily. As you read the book you will see that they form a Map.

The first part of the Map has the first four Keys, which hold the constricted poverty thinking.

```
^ ° i °   °   } °        - *  ,  /     ° -    ] ° > °
V  ^  V i'°  i °V  v V  °  >  ^v   ^ °      °
        7 i>    i } °     }
```

The second part of the Map is the most important question of all: what is your Deepest Heart wanting?

The third part of the Map contains the keys and powerful techniques for your own self-care. The principle behind them is that if you create this moment right now to be full of what you love and feel good about, as much as possible, and do that in each moment, when the future gets here it will be full of what you love.

The future is *always* getting here! In that sense, there is no future. Just the ever-unfolding present moment, moving in the DIRECTION that you are setting with your intention and self-talk about who you are and what is possible for you.

Each of these questions is deeply evocative. You could take each one in turn and explore it with your own thoughts and emotions, tapping with EFT for what comes up for you.

Another way to use this Map

I like to begin with a feeling, a body symptom or behavior, or a limiting belief, whatever is showing up most insistently to get my attention.

I fill that in on the Map, and proceed to work through the rest of the questions.

It is important to select ONE SPECIFIC experience that was challenging or painful, and good idea to give it a title.

Create the title out of the worst moment of the memory. It doesn't really matter what the title is. What counts is that when you think of it, you really feel a physical response inside.

Even though your head will want to get creative with this, or you may think "I'm no good at this!" (also your head at work!), let your body have its say here.

Go with what provokes the strongest response inside you.

Rate the intensity of feeling

Rate the intensity of your inner response - make a note of where the intensity of the feeling is on the scale of 0-10, or how ever you like to assess the intensity.

When you have completed the Map, use everything on it in your tapping session, adding any thoughts, feelings or images that come up intuitively as you go. Re-use it as often as you like, until none of the Keys on the Map bring up any negative thoughts or feelings.

On the following pages are examples of the three sections of the filled-in Map.

Please refer to the **Discovery Booklet** that accompanies this book for the 8 Master Keys Map that has blank spaces for you to use in your own search for answers, instructions how to use EFT, and many setup statements for you to use.

❋ ❋ ❋ ❋ ❋

NOTES

Profoundly light-hearted strategies for unsticking stuck stuff

The S.P.I.R.I.T.E.D. SELF

IDENTITY
I came to believe _____ about myself
(I can't be or do anything. I will mess it up.
Nothing I do is enough or good enough.
Cloudy thinking; depression)

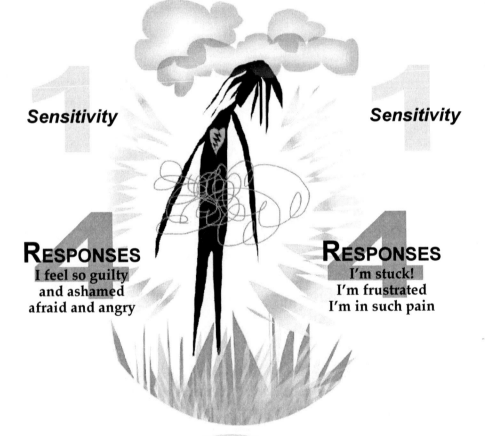

Sensitivity   *Sensitivity*

RESPONSES
I feel so guilty
and ashamed
afraid and angry

RESPONSES
I'm stuck!
I'm frustrated
I'm in such pain

PAIN-ful Experience
(Title: I'm Overwhelmed and Engulfed by My Mother's
Rage)

The S.P.I.R.I.T.E.D. SELF

INTENTION

When I feel pain, hurt
or anger, my heart is trying
to tell me that I deserve
better! I've been caging
my spirit and
**I deserve
better!**

5

Profoundly light-hearted strategies for unsticking stuck stuff

The S.P.I.R.I.T.E.D. SELF

The TRUTH about Me

I UNDERSTAND the TRUTH about me
I AM of value! I AM worthy!
I deserve to trust, love & believe in myself

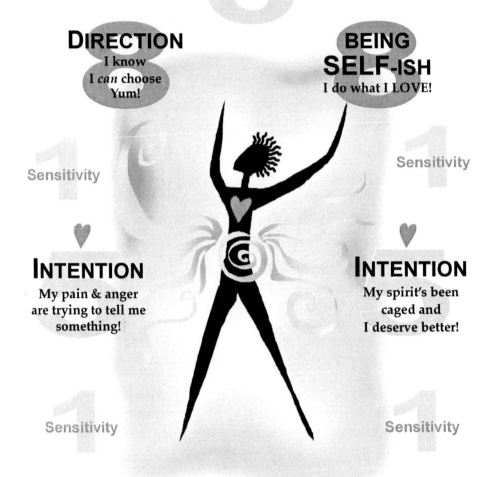

DIRECTION
I know
I *can* choose
Yum!

BEING
SELF-ISH
I do what I LOVE!

Sensitivity

Sensitivity

INTENTION
My pain & anger
are trying to tell me
something!

INTENTION
My spirit's been
caged and
I deserve better!

Sensitivity

Sensitivity

EVIDENCE of the Truth in my life

This is my Blueprint! This is Who I Am! This is where I Stand!
(Ex.: I play My music, I hold Sacred Space for my clients....)

5
YOU ARE JUST TOO SENSITIVE!

1 – Sensitivity

Begin with acknowledging your sensitivity, and tapping for your feelings about being "so sensitive."

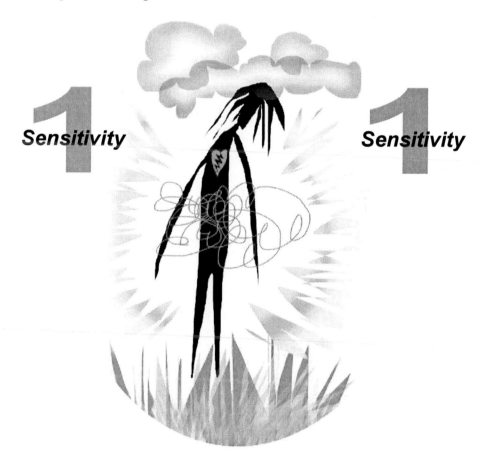

Have you ever heard
(or said about someone else):

"Oh, you are just too sensitive!"
"You take things so hard!"
"Just let it roll off your back."
"Why can't you just let it go!"
And maybe even, "What's wrong with you? You are such a cry baby!"

You have probably thought they were right—there must be something wrong!

```
             i }°  ^i^   i°   ^°
     >  °>V  >  °i    >  °   i«i>  i              ° ° °

   °L i  i i°  ° ^°  i°   `° v°>  >  i i^^°  >  °V >  °
             ^>  i°  i°   `      °
```

I speak as a "highly sensitive person" myself. It has taken me most of my life to understand this temperament and value it for its gifts. In my work as an Intuitive Mentor I have worked with many people who are extra sensitive to stress, traumatic experiences, and environmental toxins.

People with this temperament are also extraordinarily sensitive to beauty and spirituality, and they all have a desire to be a good custodian of the earth.

If you're reading this and feeling, "Yeah, that's me, all right!" *You* are the help that is on the way, whether you are sensitive yourself, or partnered/working with/interacting with/or the parent of someone who is sensitive.

Here are the email responses of a few people who have read this either in my other books or website:

when i first saw the words "sensitive person" i immediately thought, oh that's not me. but then i read on anyway, and by the end i was in tears. i think i am sensitive, and i used to get emotionally more upset about things so i learned to be hard and try to "not let things bother me." so now i have a host of some seriously debilitating health problems. now i am "tough" emotionally...(?) and sensitive physically. just reading your website has led me to some interesting ideas and thoughts about my health problems and my state of mind. M.P.

Thank you for bringing this subject into our world to the surface. I am a mom of three boys—who I believe are sensitive—which by the way, and I'm sure you know, is not accepted in society too warmly. I want them to share their gift with others and be able to attract a partner in their life that supports each other.

I was raised in a family of 9 brothers and 3 sisters. We were not allowed to show emotion in our home—my belief system tells me that it is a weakness—I tap on that everyday. I worked in a family business that supported the same feelings for 15 yrs. only to marry someone who HAD a big EGO. After 23 years of marriage—we have found EFT a valuable tool for our relationship and our family. I still battle with the effects of being sensitive and it drains my energy with/from others—I want to TAP away these beliefs so I can pass along EFT to others with confidence and conviction.   M.F.

Definitely sensitive since first grade, at least
I am now 52
Male
Have suffered panic attacks, generalized anxiety for over 29 years.
Have been suffering from mild to moderate depression on and off over half that time.
Have been to multiple psychologists, shrinks, medications include xanax, valium, clonopin, etc since I was 23.

THE 8 MASTER KEYS TO HEALING WHAT HURTS

Now just taking 1 to 2 mg clonopin a day, plus 15 to 45 mg of morphine sulphate for back pain (and I must admit, also for energy and some of the depression.)
Anyway, to cut things short, your description of a person born with a sensitive personality fits me to a tee
Unfortunately, being a male makes it even harder...so, I feel EFT really works, but I initially need some guidance .

Since I've tried in the past biofeedback, hypnotism, spiritual healers, etc, I feel EFT works the best. I'm just stuck, if you know what I mean.

You become familiar with your problems - and when I try to calm down, my body feels this stuckness is now the natural state, not calmness R.C.

I'm enjoying your first book...I know you've heard this before but I swear you're writing about me. It's scary but it helps too to realize that I'm not immature or selfish, I just feel more than most people and am hurt more easily than most. It's a very tough road, but I can't say that I'd trade for a personality that feels less. S.H.

You've helped me in so many ways, but one of the most significant ways was identifying me as highly sensitive. I no longer view myself as a high-maintenance freak.

I feel it's very OK to be as cautious and self-protective as I am and, especially, that it's not something that I have to try and get over.

I don't have to try and cure this before moving on in life because there's nothing to cure. I understand myself so much better now and that's such a good, comfortable, feeling.   M.R.

Attributes of emotionally sensitive people

From Kyra Mesich, Psy.D.

❋ They are keenly aware of the emotions of people around them.

❋ Sensitive people are easily hurt or upset. An insult or unkind remark will affect them deeply.

❋ In a similar vein, sensitive people strive to avoid conflicts. They dread arguments and other types of confrontations because the negativity affects them so much.

❋ Sensitive people are not able to shake off emotions easily. Once they are saddened or upset by something, they cannot just switch gears and forget it.

❋ Sensitive people are greatly affected by emotions they witness. They feel deeply for others' suffering. Many sensitive people avoid sad movies or watching the news because they cannot bear the weighty emotions that would drive to their core and stick with them afterwards.

❋ Sensitive people are prone to suffer from recurrent depression, anxiety or other psychological disorders.

❋ On the positive side, sensitive people are also keenly aware of and affected by beauty in art, music and nature. **They are the world's greatest artists and art appreciators.**

❋ Sensitive people are prone to stimulus overload. That is, they can't stand large crowds, loud noise, or hectic environments. They feel overwhelmed and depleted by too much stimulus.

❋ Sensitive people are born that way. They were sensitive children.

The Sensitive Person's Survival Guide • KyraMesich.com
Reprinted with permission

❋ ❋ ❋

Using the Meyers Briggs Model:

The Highly Sensitive Person is called the "Idealist Healer" (INFP)

Abstract in thought and speech
Cooperative
Introverted
Appear reserved and shy
Diplomatic
Empathic
Hunger for deep and meaningful relationships
Value personal growth, authenticity and integrity
Internally deeply caring
Deeply committed to the positive and the good
A mission to bring peace to the world
Strong personal morality
Often make extraordinary sacrifices for someone
   or something they believe in
Imagination and evolution are the goal

Seek unity, feel divided inside
Often had an unhappy childhood
May have been raised in a practical, industrious, social family
Didn't conform to parental expectations
Often feel isolated, "like an alien"

See themselves as ugly ducklings
Rich fantasy world as a child, may have been
  discouraged or punished for this by parents

Wish to please, try to hide their differences
Believe and are told that their sensitivity is bad
Drawn toward purity but continuously on the lookout for the
  wickedness they think lurks in them
Self-sacrificing to an extreme, in atonement for their failings
Keep this inner struggle hidden from others

STORIES
ABOUT SENSITIVE PEOPLE

Here are two client-stories about two very different sensitive people with very different lives. They both have resorted to numbing-out strategies to try to defend their vulnerability.

NICOLE

Nicole is a sophomore in college. She came in with her usual bright smile, but soon it became apparent that she was suffering from feelings of overwhelm in all the important areas of her life, self image, school, friends, relationships, family.

She told me that all her life she has been told that she "gets too upset." I have introduced her to the concept of the highly sensitive person. It helped her to know that there is not something wrong with her, though it is hard for her to remember that.

She continually returns to the thought that thinking there must be something wrong with her. She keeps apologizing for it.

Nicole starts out by saying she has been dieting, and she is so mad at herself about food. She is either eating or starving herself. Just this week she has had a realization—that *whenever a troubling thought or feeling comes up she reaches for something to eat to deflect her attention away from her discomfort.*

I tell her how brilliant this is! So many people go through their entire lives medicating themselves in this way with food—or sex, or work, or drugs, or smoking—and they don't ever make the connection she just did. Nicole is bemused to be called brilliant when she is describing her terrible habits, but she takes it in.

There are so many issues that Nicole feels mired in, that we begin to work with EFT on just feeling overwhelmed in general, and she bursts into tears, sobbing for a moment, but also apologizing and trying to control herself because she does not usually express how she really feels to anyone (not even to herself).

So we just tap up and down the points for a few minutes, and I come over to sit beside her to tap on her fingers while she cries and talks a bit. She is always amazed at how quickly and well EFT works.

Eventually we work on her history of being told that she "gets too upset." I ask her how it feels in her body to be so sensitive—*where does she feel that?* She says she feels it in her chest, a warm heavy feeling resting on her chest.

Often when people can't think of how to describe how something feels, I will ask questions like "Is it warmer or cooler? Is it heavier or lighter? Is it lighter or darker? Is there a color, or not? Is it a moving feeling or a still feeling?" People can almost always answer these questions. So we work with her feeling, and some specific incidents when she has felt it.

I ask her to describe the feeling.

Paradoxically, she says that even though the "too sensitive feeling" was warm and heavy on her chest, inside her it felt as if she were too light. And this feeling now of "getting too upset" is "heavier."

I talk a bit about the fact that many people overeat and gain weight because they unconsciously feel this sense of too-lightness, and want to add a sense of presence, even an intimidating presence. Consciously or unconsciously they overeat to increase their "heaviness" in the world.

Nicole is intrigued with this idea. I also tell her about orthorexia, which is a kind of reverse of overeating. Orthorexia is an obsession with eating healthy food. It is related to anorexia, but is a different eating disorder. While an anorexic wants to lose weight, *an orthorexic wants to feel pure, healthy and natural.* (Learn more at orthorexia.com)

```
      °>°>]°     i>°^°>°iiV   °v°i°
 L '] °>°>   }° °Li°" } i]» °ii° °>°
      >'^   i'fi°^«   > °^i^i
```

I say "distorted" spiritual sense, because I believe that, as human beings, we are like distilled spiritual energy, literally, "heavier" spirit. So when Nicole describes the too-sensitive feeling as heavier, I hear her saying that she is experiencing her own spiritual Presence on the earth. A sense of **spiritual Presence** is an "inside job" of beliefs, self-image, perspectives and sense of purpose.

```
      -«    > °* i^iV i° ^°>°
 ^i^i° v°vii }°v ]°v °v° i‰-î v°v]°
          >v̊ v  }  °°
```

The possibility for creative languaging is enormous here.

I ask her to fill herself deeply with this sensation.

Next I invite her to imagine having more of a sense of her Spiritual Presence in those situations where in the past she had felt "too

sensitive, as if there was something wrong with her."
We included all of this positive languaging in our rounds of tapping.

When we finished, I asked Nicole to go inside again and check out her experience of those situations, now. When she opened her eyes she said, "Well, when I see it that way, there really isn't any problem!"

RON

Nicole's experience reminds me of another session that I had many years ago with a man named Ron.

I only saw him once, but his visit left a powerful image in my mind, and taught me much about sensitivity long before I heard the term, "highly sensitive person," and before I knew EFT.

Ron came in dressed in his work clothes. I had caught sight of him outside in his truck changing his t-shirt, and his jeans showed that he worked outside. It turned out that he did construction work. In his early 40's, rugged and weathered, he was not the kind of man who usually seeks out counseling help, so I knew he must be feeling desperate.

Ron grew up in a loud, emotionally abusive, alcoholic family where there was a lot of criticism and little support. He'd had his own battles with alcohol, and with life itself.

You could see it in his worn and lined face, his quiet, sad demeanor. He was currently living in a situation where he was being unmercifully taken advantage of by his ex-wife, her teenage druggie son, AND her boyfriend—and he was supporting them all!

He thought he was being nice, and that this was what he was supposed to be doing… and he felt like he was drowning.

THE 8 MASTER KEYS TO HEALING WHAT HURTS

He had no idea how to take control of his situation. He had no experience in understanding or verbalizing what he was feeling. He was truly overwhelmed. Ron was so un-used to introspection that it took me awhile to find out how to ask him questions about himself that he could answer.

I asked him what he wanted in his life, and he had never been asked that before. He had never asked himself what he wanted. He didn't even know that it was possible to ask that question, and certainly didn't know what to say.

As a way in, I began by asking him to describe the worst things about the family he had grown up in and his situation now. That he could do. We made a long list. Then I went down the list item by item, and asked him to reverse each one.

What is the opposite of a loud environment where everyone is yelling at each other? What is the opposite of constant criticism? What is the opposite of a situation where people are always drunk and unreliable, or violent? What is the opposite of living in a place where someone always has their hand out for a handout? His responses were slow but thoughtful, and I could almost *hear* new neural pathways being formed as he tried to find feelings and images and then words for his new thoughts.

Ron and I worked through that list, and the result it produced was a revelation to him. It touched my heart to see how sensitive he was under that tough laborer exterior.

When he asked these questions of his heart, it knew the answers. That surprised him. I could see lights slowly going on inside.

Since I could see that he was such a different person than he appeared outwardly, or even knew himself, I asked him for some metaphors of what he was like "on the inside." He wasn't used to thinking symbolically, and he had mentioned a love of horses, so I asked him, "If you were a horse, what kind of horse would you be?"

And that is when his spirit started to speak. Ron described a beautiful young filly, very high-strung, scared and nervous, backed into the corner of a paddock in a meadow. She felt trapped, tense, ready to flee at the slightest movement. She could not, would not, be caught. Too terrified.

My heart in my mouth, maybe literally, I so, so gently asked him, using his experience and love of horses, did he know of a way to reach her, to touch her, to let her know that he meant her no harm.

He was in an altered state as he talked, but he did not hesitate. He described moving very very slowly, talking so softly, with such encouragement and love, taking all the time in the world to come to her. Slowly slowly putting on her halter, and gently, quietly leading her to her stall.

And then, he said, he would slowly slowly begin to pour corn into her stall, pouring and pouring until it came up over her feet… up around her legs… and up over her belly… talking softly and soothingly all the while… the grain slowly coming up to her withers… and up to her back… and finally up around her neck.

I sat spellbound, listening as he talked, feeling something begin to quiet in him, quiet and come forward. I could feel this sensation emerging in myself as well.

And then, he said, when she felt the grain all around her she would feel held, and steadied, and finally safe.   And that would change her.

A couple of weeks later I got a phone call from Ron, canceling the next appointment we had made. He said he was quitting his job, selling his house and "moving out of the area."

I took those developments as a good sign for him.…

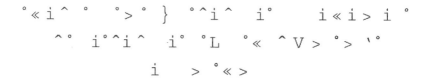

Even medical science is becoming aware of the physiological effect of emotional pain. As you read the following article, keep in mind that *emotional pain is profoundly magnified in a sensitive temperament.* So what this article describes would be even more torturous for a sensitive person.

Rejection Hurts So Bad

A Shun is as Good as a Kick in the Shins, Brain Study Finds

by Amanda Gardner, HealthDay Reporter

THURSDAY, Oct. 9, 2003 (HealthDayNews) - If you feel like you've been punched in the stomach after your lover walks out on you, that may be because that is what it feels like.

Researchers at the University of California at Los Angeles (UCLA), publishing in the Oct. 10 issue of Science, have found that emotional pain and physical pain can stimulate the same parts of the brain.

Thirteen participants were hooked up to functional magnetic resonance imaging (fMRI) equipment while they played a ball tossing video game called Cyberball. The fMRI monitors blood flow to different parts of the brain.

The experiment involved three different scenarios. In the first, participants were told they could only watch, not play, due to technical difficulties ("nobody's fault" exclusion). In the second scenario, the participants played ball with two other "players" (actually the computer). In the third and final scenario, the two "players" who started threw the ball only to each other, intentionally excluding the third participant.

THE 8 MASTER KEYS TO HEALING WHAT HURTS

There were blood flow changes in two areas of the brain. Flow was increased to the anterior cingulated cortex, which has previously been associated with the experience of physical pain. The right ventral prefrontal cortex, however was activated when the distress was least, indicating that it might actually work to counteract the feeling of being shunned.

There is an evolutionary reason for this finely tuned system: Mammals need their mothers. And when their mothers (or the rest of the social group) are not there, the brain sends out an urgent message.

"There are various things in the world that humans need in order to survive, and the ones we typically think of are to avoid physical harm," says senior study author Matthew Lieberman, an assistant professor of psychology at UCLA. "For human beings and mammals more generally, being socially connected is just as important. You are more likely to die as a result of social exclusion than of physical pain." Naomi Eisenberger, a graduate student at UCLA, was the lead author of the paper.

"We think this part of the brain functions as an alarm system telling the conscious, logical, willful part of the brain that it's time to turn its attention to some problem," Lieberman adds.

For 21st century mammals, what this means is that social support systems are good for us. "Emotional pain is an undesired psychological state of affairs, and the less there is of that in social networks, the more harmoniously people will interact," Jaak Panksepp, author of an accompanying perspective article, told a group of reporters. "Coming to terms with the true nature of emotional feelings in the brain is essential for constructing the kinds of social institutions and habits that can optimize human and animal welfare."

It may also convince rationalists to pay more attention to the emotional side of life. "We tend to think of social pain as not as real as physical pain," Lieberman says. "

THE 8 MASTER KEYS TO HEALING WHAT HURTS

At a minimum, this suggests that social pain isn't as imaginary, that it's actually rooted in this deep evolutionary process, and that it's a critical part of survival for children. It may not be critical for survival for adults in some objective sense, but because we've now evolved, we feel terrible when this alarm goes off."

The next step would be to look at how social support systems can mitigate these painful effects. "It would be important to see how social comfort actually changes pain-induced distress, and which types of pain it can modulate," Panksepp told HealthDay in a separate interview.

The study has an eerie, real-life counterpart in the story of the New York City man, Antoine Yates, who was housing a 425-pound tiger in his apartment.

The tiger was taken to a wildlife refuge in Ohio after mauling his owner's leg. Noting the separation from his beloved if fearsome pet, Yates told the New York Daily News, "The pain in my leg is nothing compared to the pain to my heart."

Or maybe the two are more alike than he realizes.

Hopefully, Yates has loved ones who can ease his hurt. The tiger, meanwhile, is too ferocious to be placed with other tigers. Caretakers are hoping he'll calm down enough so that he, too, can have a support system.

More information

For more information on bullying, a form of social exclusion, visit **the American Academy of Child and Adolescent Psychiatry** or **Bullying.org**.

And to learn about what hurts, try **the American Pain Foundation**.

SOURCES: Matthew Lieberman, Ph.D., assistant professor,

psychology, University of California, Los Angeles; Jaak Panksepp, Ph.D., professor emeritus, Bowling Green State University, Bowling Green, Ohio, and head, affective neuroscience research, Falk Center for Molecular Therapeutics, Northwestern University, Evanston, Ill.; Oct. 10, 2003, Science

Charlotte Bronte: highly sensitive

The following is some interesting speculation about sensitivity sent to me by an alert and thoughtful client:

Rue, I suspect that Charles Dickens could be added to the list of highly sensitive people. He certainly created enough characters in his books that I would consider highly sensitive. This takes into account that in his time, women, at least high-born women, were considered to be delicate and of highly sensitive natures.

In his books we find low-born women who are highly sensitive, as well as men who, regardless of their class, would be considered highly sensitive. I would include in this category people who are described as keenly aware of the feelings of others, people who are highly sensitive to their surroundings, people who are highly attuned to the beauties of nature, and people who are easily hurt by the influence of people around them. Many of his characters also show highly intuitive natures.

Most of Dickens' main characters are highly sensitive people. They spend much of their time being hounded by highly *insensitive* people who make their lives very difficult. However, the HSP's triumph at the end, usually after having to go through arduous trials and tribulations and overcome the *insensitive* people. But they never compromise their highly sensitive natures, and in the end win out, while the insensitive folks generally come to a bad end.

I cannot begin to tell you how highly sensitive a person Charlotte Bronte was. Actually it seems like the entire family of six children was highly sensitive (two died very young). The other four were each other's companions entirely. They rarely left the parsonage where they lived, which was in a tiny village right on the edge of the Yorkshire moors.

They were very unaccustomed to visitors, and I think you could probably say that their HSPness was both genetic and environmental. Today we would call them shy. They were terrified of meeting strangers, and physically they were not robust.

I am reading a biography of Charlotte. Once she became famous she had to go to London to see her publishers, meet other writers, etc. These trips were extremely difficult for her, because of her fear of meeting new people and of being in new environments. An example from the book is one social event where there were to be not more than 12 people. Charlotte spent the entire day with a headache just in anticipation of the evening, and afterwards she probably could not get to sleep because of the excitement brought on by the event.

Her life became even more difficult after she and her father had to bury two sisters, Anne and Emily, and their brother in less than a year. And it was Charlotte who cared for them, nursed them, and was at their bedsides when they died.

How she survived this I don't know, except that she had very strong religious beliefs which comforted her, and she had developed a very strong, disciplined character which got her through the most trying of times, but she often was made sick by weather changes, having to meet new people, and dealing with the outside world due to her literary career. J.F.

NOTES

6
WHAT BROKE YOUR HEART?

Sensitivity *Sensitivity*

PAIN-ful Experience

(Title: I'm Overwhelmed and Engulfed by My Mother's Rage)

2 – Painful Experience
A powerful memory that lies frozen in the past.

Most of us don't have any problem coming up with painful memories! We are less familiar with the experience of being in the throes of one of our most effective limiting behaviors, or suffering from a physical pain, and at the same time having the presence of mind to ask ourselves what might be the origin, deep in the past, of our feeling this way today.

If you are feeling overwhelmed by what is going on in your life and how you feel about it, and you can't even begin to think of where to start with EFT, try asking yourself some powerful and evocative questions:

What broke your heart?
When did something die in you, get blocked, shut down?

Write out or tape yourself talking about your experiences. Then take each of the sentences of your story or journal entry that carries a charge for you, and turn it into a tapping sequence.

Go deeper.

Ask yourself: What did I lose as a result?

A painful experience makes us feel that we have lost our sense of connection, belonging, safety, peace, joy, integrity, wholeness.

Honor yourself for how hard this has been, and tap for this deep loss.

Here are some more deep and evocative questions that will help you get to the key experiences in your life that are asking for healing:

❋ What does this remind me of?

❊ If I could live life over again, what person or event would I prefer to skip?

❊ When was the last time I cried, and why?

❊ Who/what makes me angry, and why?

❊ What is my biggest sadness or regret?

❊ What is missing to make my life perfect?

❊ Name 3 fears I would rather not have.

❊ What do I wish I had never done?

Ashe's story:

Ashe took one of my four-week teleclasses, and had bravely volunteered to be a tapping demonstration subject. She hadn't shared a lot of her story during the class, but since her tapping sessions over the weeks seemed quite profound and useful to her, I asked later if she would share a little about her background, and how the class had affected her.

Her answer demonstrates the power of what happens to us as children, and how it shapes our adult behavior.

I am so grateful for her willingness to share this, and as always, honored when someone offers their story.
These tales of pain and transformation become a guiding light for the healing of all of us.

ASHE

I don't want to be like my mother and I am so much like her it's not funny.

Profoundly light-hearted strategies for unsticking stuck stuff

I feel like a small child frozen in fear.

My mother was a teacher who *always* played the teacher. Whatever I wanted to do she always said I was too young. To any of my child wisdom she would say in a derogative tone, "What would you know? You're only a child," even though I was proved right time and time again. I've cleared heaps around her but nothing seems to touch this fear of doing what I am drawn to and love doing, and my fear of "standing alone."

That violent crazy side of her has terrified me and what it boils down to is I'm terrified of both doing and being, because I don't want to be like her.

That started when I was very little. So I started being like my dad, which was controlling, numbing the feelings ...effectively not-being. Appearing calm on the outside at all costs...because otherwise she'd "get you" energetically once she started, and then you'd end up being wrong and punished and the "whipping post" for her to vent on.

It required a huge amount of control not to respond, because I was so sensitive and felt all that so much. Until very recently I always got scared around overdoing things and being tired, because I would lose my patience (read shutting down, steely tolerance and jaw-locking self-control), and when I was little that meant being shamed big time.

This whole thing obviously touched off something in her that scared her too, because she couldn't deal with my reaction. Whenever I was angry she told me I was tired. The result was that by the time I was a teenager I got glandular fever and ended up permanently tired...until I started clearing my anger.

An incident with her when I was much smaller (age 2 to 3) came up where she "lost it" and it was so terrifying I disappeared. It was as if all there was, was her raging terror. I can see from my perspective now, that this was a frozen moment of raging fear that has been passed down the generations in my family for who knows how long. I am the first to acknowledge it, let alone deal with it. My grandmother got Alzheimer's rather than deal with her version of it.

When I was little my mother visited a lady who was in and out of mental hospitals, I'm sure to make herself feel sane by comparison. Nothing wrong with OUR family...only other people's families had problems...people who were too stupid to help themselves. My mother would go and piously try to help some poor unfortunate families!

This is another fear. I really want to help people but not like that !!!!! All I could do with that was surrender it to a higher force and open my heart to both of us, and ask for it to be healed.

Yesterday I felt very edgy, and without knowing why, I started picking on my husband and getting really angry with him. I was watching it too. At that point I started to notice how scared and unreasonable I was being, and I started to pay even more attention. It was as if a cold bony hand was gripping the inside of my stomach.

I realized that having this feeling inside herself was exactly what had made my mother pick on me and tell me all the horrible things that were wrong with me. So again, all I could do in that moment was surrender it and ask for grace to open my heart to myself and her.

I noticed some time back that I could only use my energy in defiance. That wasn't how I wanted to do things any more, but I had no way of being with ease.

All my inner knots are unraveling nicely now as fast as I can process, and your course and EFT have helped immensely. Things just popped out so easily. It was really such a great help to work from a different perspective. I felt very safe with you.

So this is about where I'm up to and a bit dazed by the whole thing, but open to a new way of being and doing things that I know is already there waiting for me to be ready and open to it.

THE 8 MASTER KEYS TO HEALING WHAT HURTS

I've already experienced this many times, but the fear of this stuff was there too so I couldn't trust or love what I thought of as myself.

❋ ❋ ❋

There are several themes in Ashe's story that will recur through this book:

❋ Painful experiences are felt more deeply by a sensitive person, especially a child.

❋ Painful experiences lead to beliefs about who we are and what is possible for us in life.

❋ It may not be possible or safe to express the powerful anger, sadness and fear and shame that we feel during and after these painful experiences.

❋ Those feelings get "stuffed" or swallowed.

❋ The stuffed feelings show up later in our lives as physical and emotional pain and illness.

❋ The people in our families who mistreated us did so because this is how they had been treated, and these were the beliefs and feelings they themselves took on.

❋ The tendency to replicate these beliefs and feelings and illnesses gets passed on down through the generations of a family.

❋ The fear of confronting the powerful feelings stops us from beginning a healing journey.

Our personal healing can heal the whole family history.

EFT is an effective tool!

I want to share with you the first set in the compilation of emails between "Leila" and me from our sessions over the course of a year. I have been deeply inspired by her heartfelt and articulate words, the strength of her willingness to do EFT, and her courage to face the painful and harrowing experiences in her history.

Leila is a real tribute to what is possible with EFT. You will hear more of her story later in this book.

Leila began by sending me a long account of her childhood and young adulthood. This is a much-shortened version:

LEILA

My story begins as the oldest child of a mother who suffered from serious postpartum depression, though in those days it wasn't diagnosed, and even today my mother won't acknowledge it. Her wounds were deep and that made her a distant, unhappy and angry mother. Our reality was a serious existence punctuated by outbursts and tears from mom and no explanations of anything from either parent.

At some point they had agreed to not discuss their differences in front of the children, and since they disagreed about virtually everything—we grew up in a vacuum—no television, no radio, no religion, no moral guidance, no interaction between our parents and very little allowed between each other.

We each lived in our own isolated little world, controlled by fear of our mother's temper and tears.

Dad was a young dentist working for Public Health and being transferred around Canada. We moved 6 times in my first 10 years. Mom was angry our whole childhood. She had difficult childbirths and was allergic to the anesthetic during her C-sections. Her fourth child, born when I was 8, was conceived after mom had her tubes tied, and her anger and resentment were enormous.

We think that she may have presumed that by marrying a young dentist she would be lifted from her prairie poverty roots to a higher level in society. Instead she ended up isolated with her ever-increasing babies, uprooted and moved almost every year for the first 10 years of her marriage.

Dad was distant, and still suffering the after-effects of WWII, where, though he wasn't physically injured, the horror of dropping enormous bombs on German cities, and not knowing at which moment he and his 5-man crew would become one of the planes that didn't return to base in England next morning, took a huge toll on his emotional availability.

So Mom was very isolated and angry. Instead of being elevated into higher society she had to accept that her mother-in-law, a gentle Irish music teacher, had no interest in climbing society's ladder. My grandmother was a quiet, shy woman, busy caring for her mentally handicapped son, my dad's older brother, the surviving twin of a difficult childbirth.

My mother's resentment was shocking.

Even without television and radio to help us form our opinions, we knew that something was terribly wrong with her. Dad was old-fashioned and never spoke a bad word of her and we were taught by example to do the same.

In fact, dad's unspoken messages and disappointment with his situation (and me) possibly did more damage to my young soul than mom's outright anger and inability to love her daughters.

Years later, I have come to understand that much of my ability to withstand abuse came from dad's unspoken messages that I was a disappointment, and that I had to toughen up. Part of toughening up was learning to handle mom's outbursts. As a consequence, as an adult, when men would berate me and mistreat me it felt very familiar and deserved. I was unable to stand up for myself.

My parents did not intentionally set out
to create an icy environment for their children to grow up in.

Circumstances created a difficult marriage for them and they stuck it out. Being the oldest, I was particularly aware of how cold their marriage was, especially as I got older and ventured out into my friends' and cousins' homes.

Not speaking of the obvious differences in the warmth and interaction found in their homes and ours was another of dad's unspoken laws – and we silently obeyed, other than a few teenage outbursts quickly quelled by mom's outrage and slaps.

Mom's hands, though gentle when we were sick (she had been trained as a nurse), were something to be feared. Somehow, for reasons we may never know, mom's rage was her strongest emotion. It was in her hands, and for other reasons we may never know, she was unable to balance her rage with loving care.

Writing about this now, makes the little girl in me feel such loneliness and need for affection.

In recent years I have had to learn how to give that little girl the loving she deserves, but of course for many years I had no idea what was wrong with me, and after my first marriage (which was a good one), became involved with men who took advantage of my need. They themselves were products of difficult childhoods and our dysfunctions brought us together, in fact, attracted us to each other and did a lot of damage to my first marriage, to myself and to my children.

A call for help

Leila's very-first-email-on-a-computer-in-her-life was her first email to me, asking if I could help her!

Saturday February 5. My first e-mail on a computer ever. A long hard trail has brought me here. All my senses are telling me this is right where I'm supposed to go. I hope you can help. I have very little money so how can I get help? I've read and reread (Dr. John) Sarno books about pain and have read and reread Freedom from Fibromyalgia by Dr. Nancy Selfridge, but I can't concentrate long enough to put them into practice.

It's been 10 years since being diagnosed with fibromyalgia and post traumatic stress syndrome. I've been treated with various medications which all produced serious negative side effects, including one two-year period of struggling to overcome the effects of accidentally being taken off a high dose of an antidepressant suddenly.

I seem to be allergic to all usual pain medications so am on a tiny dose of methadone: 3ml per day, and zopiclone at night (11mg). I have been determined to stay as clear of drugs as possible. In all my readings, John Sarno and Nancy Selfridge sound to me to be the truth. This Christmas my daughter got a computer, and today I found you through Nancy's name. It is unbelievable that I can reach out for help like this. Would you be able to talk to me?

I suggested that Leila download Gary Craig's free manual on the Emofree.com website (I told her how to do it), and begin to practice on her own, first. Most of the subsequent and considerable healing work that Leila has done has been on her own. We have worked together a few times on the phone.

Leila has a great determination to create her life differently. Now she is studying to be a resource for others, including being a practitioner of EFT. She is a natural healer.

Leila began to come up with her own tapping routines created from her insights and the few telephone sessions that we did.

Profoundly light-hearted strategies for unsticking stuck stuff

As our work progressed, she often sent me long, eloquent emails about how EFT and other events in her life were bringing her to a remarkable new awakening to her real potential, and healing her pain once and for all, to her astonishment and even the surprise of her doctor, who seemed to think there was nothing more he could do for her.

Of her profoundly challenging story, the following messages are a sampling of what she wrote. Leila's story is so compelling that I have encouraged her to write it into a book of her own!

A beginning with EFT

Dear Rue, How are you? I've been working hard here, when I can, to start using EFT. Thank you for getting me started. I was so overwhelmed at first.

At the same time, I've been working from Nancy's book on Fibromyalgia. I had read it many times, but was having trouble retaining anything long enough to put it into practice. So now I'm actually doing some of the exercises for the first time. At the same time, I'm doing EFT for the first time. So I go back and forth between the two.

Some days I have no energy at all for it and some days the pain is too much - but overall I'm making progress.

Today I got through my early childhood - up to about age 8 - there was a lot of difficult stuff there - but I tapped my way through it - a few each day.

I haven't tapped through the events in 1983 (I would have been 30 years old then) when one of my children was shot and killed. I started to—but was unable.

THE 8 MASTER KEYS TO HEALING WHAT HURTS

That's OK for now—I have enough on my plate dealing with things chronologically. Every day is different here - dealing with life's daily challenges plus the pain and foggy brain.

I do feel better though. Doing the work in my childhood has helped me see that my mother probably had what they now call post partum depression (in her case possibly psychosis) - but in those days they didn't talk about it. So that has helped me have some compassion and understanding even though to this day, she refuses to admit she ever did anything wrong and blames our difficult childhood on our father.

So now I know how to put that into a sequence....

Even though my mother can't admit any wrong-doing, I deeply and completely love and accept myself and am open to healing the situation now.

What a blessing this is.

The e-mails and newsletters that come from Gary Craig completely overwhelm me. I'm not healthy enough yet to focus long enough to take much of this in. I have to keep this simple.

My pain level is still high even after doing all this work. For pain I'm only taking 2ml per day of methadone, so sometimes it gets pretty bad—but that's OK—

I'm sure if I keep working on this a breakthrough will come.

Working on Nancy's book takes a lot of time and really tests my ability to concentrate—learning self-talk, visualization, meditation, and journaling—but I'm slowly starting to do them all.

I'm very grateful to have the time and space in my life at this moment to do this. I've been waiting for my youngest child to graduate to do this work on myself, but the pain has gotten to be too much—so away I go—always keeping in mind that my daughter still always comes first while she slugs her way through Grade 12.

If you have any suggestions it would be wonderful to hear from you. I find your words very comforting and helpful. In fact hearing from you on this computer has helped to create a huge breakthrough for me—like a miracle. Thank you.

Sincerely, Leila

Starting in early childhood

With the EFT program, I've started the Basic Recipe, starting at the very beginning of my journaling—doing three painful memories a day—starting in early childhood. I haven't gotten very far yet - again because of the pain and the fog and life's other demands. But I'm on track and working on it.

I do have some serious issues in my life—starting with being the oldest of 4 children of a mother who suffered from serious post-partum depression—(though she hasn't admitted it.) By starting in my childhood, I'm assuming that chronological order is the best, but I could be wrong. The worst stuff comes later, and is so bad I can't touch it without serious pain. That's where I need help.

There are a lot of bad things. The instant help you offered to me when I e-mailed you a couple of weeks ago makes me trust that it's OK to write down the worst of it for you, though usually I keep it out of my mind. Please understand I have to treat this with a lot of reverence. It is a very long story, with much trauma both before and after this event.

I do not like to hold this up like a "ticket" or a "badge" for the degree of trauma - do you understand? I know you do. For years I didn't sleep at all - which is what led to the fibromyalgia in the first place. My FEARS have always been more hyper than normal. My vigilance

Profoundly light-hearted strategies for unsticking stuck stuff

started even before I had babies—watching out for mom's mood swings—being the oldest and watching out for the others—one attempt by an uncle at sexual molestation when I was around 5—in the dark, in my bed...

My baby Jerry (my third child) was born in March 1981, and my baby Noah was born in May 1983 - then baby Noah was killed in August 1983.

(NOTE: I have edited the details of this story out here. It is truly horrific and none of us needs the images from it in our imaginations. The fact that Leila has survived and is thriving now is such a testament to how strong the human spirit really is, and how possible it is to heal from what has happened to us.)

The shock of the shooting and the memories of all the violence and trying to sort out the brainwashing and the continuing fear all combined to keep me virtually sleepless for years. I was ever-vigilant.

I carried on like a soldier. I'm very strong, and a lot has happened to me—more trauma—and finally the price for being so strong was fibromyalgia and post traumatic stress syndrome.

There were many years of lonely lonely times for me with much much guilt, and then the pain and extreme fatigue—diagnosed with fibromyalgia in 1993, but I kept working at home support until 2000—dealing with many many very serious issues that kept me awake nights until I finally became unable to cope with the sleeplessness and finally asked for medication to help (1994).

The medication only gave me about 4 - 5 hours sleep and that gradually diminished as my body grew accustomed to it. Finally this year (2005)—a couple of months ago—I made the decision to get off it and am very happy that I did. I am finally getting some natural sleep—mostly thanks to EFT and my work with you - and my nights are much better.

Resistance is the key

Dear Rue, I just had an amazing breakthrough realization. This strong *resistance* to spending the time *doing the work* can only be some form of addiction. Addiction to what?? Addiction to negative brain chemistry!!

As soon as the body realizes it may have to give up its years of familiar brain chemicals it throws up a huge block of resistance. Of course. The solution?? The tried and true formula for all addictions. The 12 Step program.

"Admitted I was powerless over my negative brain chemistry and that my life had become unmanageable!!!!!"

"Came to believe that a power greater than myself could restore me to my sanity!!!"

All the way through step by step to:
"Humbly asked Him to remove our shortcomings."

God please help me with this addiction to negative brain chemistry. It is a very strong addiction. I can't break it by myself. It has taken over and makes my life unmanageable and it is hurting myself and others.

Many addictions have been cured by the 12 Step program. And there is every reason to believe that EFT will work on an addiction to body chemistry. Don't know why I haven't thought of it before.

I'll let you know how things change now for me.
!!!

Dear Rue, How are you? I am doing much better. Your set of e-mails has really helped.

First, I had to deal with my body's addiction to the chemicals my brain produces when I'm in negative thinking or fear.

So I put that into step one of the twelve steps and did all the steps on it. That really helped.

Then I took "addiction to negative thinking and fear" and put that into the suggestions from you.

"I release my addiction to negative thinking and fear (two different things really) to my Higher Power to transform it and my relationship to it, never to take it back or passively receive it back," and I did the tapping.

I'm much more relaxed about this now and feel more like an artist than a robot doing the tapping. (Plus I'm much more gentle with myself.)

Then I went through all the EFT points, tapping for sadness, fear, shame, embarrassment, hurt, grief, guilt, pain, anger, and trauma, then the forgiveness steps.

Then brought in my Higher Power to fill up the empty spaces.

Then I wrote out the Gratitude Diet and tapped on it.

The only one I had trouble with is the second one—"I am grateful for all my experiences and what they have taught me" because of how many people I have hurt—especially my children. All the rest of them I feel good about.

I feel a lot better. I'll keep working on this—

Love from Leila

THE FIRE IN THE SONG
by David Whyte

The mouth opens
and fills the air
with its vibrant shape

until the air
and the mouth
become one shape

And the first word
your own word
spoken from that fire

surprises, burns
grieves you now
because

you made that pact
with the dark presence
in your life

He said, "If you only
stop singing
I'll make you safe"

And he repeated the line,
knowing you would hear
"I'll make you safe"

as the comforting
sound of a door
closed on the fear at last,

but his darkness crept
  under your tongue
   and became the dim

cave where
  you sheltered
   and grew

in that small place
  too frightened to
remember
   the songs of the world,

its impossible notes,
  and the sweet joy
   that flew out the door

of your wild mouth
  as you spoke

- David Whyte
from *"Fire in the Earth"*
used with permission from **Many Rivers Press**, 1992

❋ ❋ ❋ ❋ ❋

7
THE CAGE OF MY AWAKENING

IDENTITY
I came to believe _____ about myself
(I can't be or do anything. I will mess it up.
Nothing I do is enough or good enough.
Cloudy thinking; depression)

Sensitivity   *Sensitivity*

PAIN-ful Experience
(Title: I'm Overwhelmed and Engulfed by My Mother's Rage)

3 – Identity:

From this experience, what did you learn to believe about yourself, or about how it would be for you in the world? (See next page for Map.)

Tapas Fleming, developer of Tapas Acupressure Technique, has said that fibromyalgia is the result of the feeling of helplessness arising in abusive situations. She says it is about the belief that, "I can't resist anything."

Experiences Lead to Beliefs...
...Lead to Feelings…
...Can Lead to Illness and Pain....

This is a simple sounding equation with profound consequences. Here is a story to illustrate it:

SHAUNA

"Shauna" has fibromyalgia. Shauna's challenges began early—she was potty trained at 9 months—with a belt. She grew up with severe phobias, especially a phobia about not making it to the bathroom. Her mother had been pregnant with her before her parents were married, but that was a family secret that she didn't learn until she was nearly 50.

I was the trial case. If I was perfect who could say anything about what they had done? The feeling from my mother was: You have to be what I need you to be. You can't have any needs. So I was completely out of touch with what I wanted or needed.

On my report card the teachers always wrote that I was painfully shy. I wasn't shy—I was terrified of doing the wrong thing. I didn't have friends. No clue. Because I couldn't be anyone. It is hard to have a friend if you are no one. I ended up being kind of cute and smart but serious. Man, I was one serious camper.

I never felt smart enough. Never felt like a smart person. Expectations kill me. I am angry about them.

We can imagine Shauna as a little baby, long before she had words to think about this experience with, and long before she was able to look at her parents' lives and determine whether this was reasonable behavior on their part. (not that potty training with a belt would ever be reasonable!)

It makes sense that she grew up with beliefs like:

* I have to be perfect
* I can't have my own needs
* I am terrified of doing the wrong thing
* I am no one
* I am not smart enough
* Expectations kill me.

These beliefs would have been unconsciously held, at first. As we saw in the last chapter, it is quite likely that Shauna's mother had this kind of upbringing, and similar beliefs. So as Shauna's life unfolded she would have had a ready lens though which to interpret her experiences as evidence.

Slowly, her unconscious beliefs would emerge into her consciousness, but she would have experienced them as "who I am:" her identity. It didn't occur to her to question them.

And we can imagine that in her life, especially as a child, it was never possible or safe to express—or even feel—her anger. It would have been stuffed and buried inside, so deeply that she would not even be aware of it. Eventually, her body began to hurt.

As that escalated, Shauna sought medical help, and got caught up in years of seeing experts, being diagnosed, treated with multiple drugs. Some of this treatment helped, but she didn't heal. As she said, "Expectations kill me."

The Cage of My Awakening

(This eloquent statement was written to me in an email by a telephone client, a man who lives in another state.)

I have been trapped inside a cage since high school.
A cage of retarded emotional development, locked, frozen.

Unable to cope in my relations with other humans. Unable to appropriately process the feelings and emotions that naturally occur during the course of those relations. Unable to appreciate the good feelings. Unable to let go of the bad feelings and move on.
As the bad feelings have accumulated it hasbeen harder and harder to feel any good feelings and harder yet to let go of the bad feelings.

I have drifted from shallow friendship to shallow friendship
to the point where the comfort of strangers is more rewarding than that of close friends, for each of my friends has been the source of a hurt that I have stored up inside.

To the point now where the bars of this cage have become so solid and rigid and the keys of the door thrown away and lost forever. It has taken pain and grief on a scale as great as the pain and grief that I experienced in high school to give me the impetus and strength to get up off the floor and throw my weight against that door.

And throw it I will.

Again and again until it shatters beneath my weight and I break out into the light to enjoy life once more a free man.

The freedom I have been seeking all these years has been misnamed and misunderstood by me. It is not freedom from responsibility but freedom from the oppressive emotional burden that I have carried around all these years.

In fact freedom IS responsibility.

And thus I have reached my time of awakening.

❋ ❋ ❋ ❋ ❋

Tiger in a Cage

It comes as a reaction to experiences that have befallen us. Our physical and emotional reaction to those experiences is a message to ourselves that we are not caring for ourselves as fully, as deeply, as profoundly as we deserve.

These early experiences led us to believe that we were not worthy of attention and caring, even our own. We began to form limiting beliefs about our selves that slowly receded into our unconscious minds, and eventually felt so familiar that we now think this is actually who we are.

But our bodies carry for us all those thoughts and feelings that we couldn't, maybe still can't, speak or act upon, have never forgotten.

We are contained in our belief system.

Neurologist Bessel van der Kolk says, "The body keeps the score."

From Carolyn Myss: "Our biology is our biography."

Gary Craig frames working with EFT to deal with limiting beliefs as "cutting off the table legs" that hold up these beliefs, or cutting down the trees in the forest. Being a sensitive person, I was always a little bit bothered by the idea of cutting forests down or chopping off table legs, so I've created a metaphor that works better for me.

I use the metaphor of a cage. Our limiting beliefs keep us caged in a smaller space that we can move comfortably in—but it is dangerously, comfortably familiar.

I think of the story I heard once about the tiger in the San Diego Zoo. I don't know if this is a true story or not, but it has stuck in my

For credits, please see list of contributors at the end of this book

mind for years as a wonderful metaphor of how we limit ourselves. Historically, in zoos, animals were kept in cages.

For the same reason I can't go to the Humane Society, I can't go to the zoo, because I always imagine being the animal that is caged, and it's too painful. As you know, the old zoos had small cages, even for big wild animals like tigers.

The San Diego Zoo had a huge, magnificent tiger in one of their cages. All this tiger could do was pace within the cage bars, even after the cage was removed. Scientists have studied animals in zoos, and found out that the caged animals experience the same kinds of depression, emotional illnesses and chronic pain and immune system challenges that humans do. So thankfully, people have begun to pay more attention to how we are treating our animal co-walkers on the earth.

When I read Tara Brach's book *Radical Acceptance*, I discovered that she told the same story about a tiger in a zoo, but it took place in a different location than the one I had heard, with a different tiger.

The story Tara Brach tells is about a magnificent white tiger named Mohini, who was kept in the Washington D.C. Zoo. There she was, this beautiful tiger in this cage, and she would walk back and forth, back and forth—twelve feet this way, twelve feet that way, twelve feet this way, day after day.

Eventually a beautiful tiger environment was built around Mohini's cage, which had hills and valleys and water and greenery and all good things that tigers like. (Except, of course, freedom…) When the environment was complete, they dismantled the cage around her. To their surprise she continued to pace twelve feet this way, twelve feet that way, twelve feet this way, measuring out with her steps what she believed was her limitation.

I don't know if she was ever able to expand into the space that was

Profoundly light-hearted strategies for unsticking stuck stuff

available to her. She was caged by her experience, the habit of her belief that the cage was still around her. I think that we are like that. We all have limiting beliefs that imprison us, cage us. Each of the bars of the cage has been created by an experience in our lives, usually early in life, when we don't have the experience or ability to think about what it really means.

We may decide that that look, or that tone of voice, or how he treated me, or what she did (or didn't) do means that we are "bad," or not lovable, or not enough. When experiences like this become more and more familiar, we begin to think that they are the truth about us.

The bars begin to come up all around us, and soon we can only pace back and forth within our limiting beliefs. Like a magnet, we attract to ourselves more experiences like those early painful ones, experiences that just reinforce what we fear is true about us.

When the human spirit is caged or limited or obstructed or blocked, it suffers. I believe that there is in all of us a deep knowing of our worth and value, and a deep love of freedom and choice, possibility, of creative expression.

We all have adopted, probably unconsciously, a cage or two to live in. It has become familiar and even sort of comfortable, in the way that something unknown is more scary than what is known, even if what is known is awful.

Now there is a conflict inside us. There is a difference of opinion between what we think is true, and what *really* is true about us—that we no longer remember, or maybe never even knew because the people around us didn't know it about themselves, and so weren't able to mirror it back to us. The inner conflict generates emotions of anger, fear, sadness.

"You only have to look at a bird in a cage and ask the question 'why do birds have wings?' The rest follows."

- *Virginia McKenna*, Born Free Founder and Trustee

Zoos are Not Beyond Reproach

Even the "best" zoos are far from being beyond reproach.

Vicki Croke, in her book, *The Modern Ark, The Story of Zoos: Past, Present and Future* (Scribner, 1997), wrote,

"Zoo officials vehemently disagree, but according to a recent survey conducted by the Born Free Foundation (a British charity that monitors animals in captivity), mental illness among zoo animals is rampant. Somewhat anecdotal, the 1993 study took three years to complete and involved one hundred zoos.

"The group says it found a bulimic gorilla in Barcelona, bulimic chimps in Sacramento, a psychotic baboon in Cyprus and a bear that constantly pulled its hair out in Rome. The director of the study said, 'Our evidence confirms that, deprived of their natural environment, social structures and outlets for many of the skills for which they have naturally evolved, animals exhibit abnormal behavior.'"

She points out that it is "easy" for zoo defenders to shrug off such criticism as coming from "untrained observers." But then she points to the opinion of the curator of mammals of the National Zoo, Washington, D.C., who, in an article published in *Zoo Biology* in 1991, claimed that a review of the literature revealed that "fully 60 percent of captive bears perform stereotypic behavior".

Stereotypic behavior, the mindless and sometimes self-destructive repetitions in a behavior, is indicative of serious mental disorder. It is also familiar to any observant zoo visitor.

Croke describes the visit of Dr. Nicholas Dodman, a brain chemistry expert at Tuft's University School of Veterinary Medicine, to the San Diego Zoo in 1994 with his family. While everyone else was awed by the vast array of spectacular creatures, the scientist says he was shocked by this "stereotyper's heaven." Everywhere he looked, he saw bears pacing, elephants swaying and giraffes bobbing their heads.

Dodman claims at least 30 percent—and perhaps as much as 50 percent—of the animals he observed at the San Diego Zoo were indulging in this disturbing activity. His impulse, he says, was to move to San Diego to study the phenomenon, but he quickly realized that "you could go to any zoo and see the same thing."

And Dogs Need to Be Dogs

Dr. Andrew Luescher of Purdue University, who is conducting research into MRI image scanning of canines with compulsive disorders, says the same thing applies with dogs.

"In people with compulsive disorders, you have very characteristic changes in the brain," he says. "So we think it will be the same in dogs.

"Two of the main reasons that dogs become stressed and anxious are when they can't predict what's going to happen and don't have control over what's happening. Their environment is inconsistent. They're left alone at home, and they develop separation anxiety. So they start chewing or digging."

From *Best Friends Animal Sanctuary*
BestFriends.org

What Keeps *People* in Cages?

It makes me so sad to see animals unable to be who they really are, existing only to be stared at, or maybe even experimented on. There is plenty of research suggesting that caging an animal can lead to depression and illness. We humans are the same. Living in our cages of limiting beliefs leads to depression and illness as well.

Why would great powerful tigers like ourselves stay in a cage?

We stay there, in our cages, pacing nervously back and forth, filled with repressed rage and grief, for lots of reasons:
The cage is familiar, all we have known.
It is safe.
It is at least safer, we think, than venturing into the unknown.

In my first marriage, in ignorance of what was possible for me, I thought of murder but never divorce. Divorce did not happen in my family! I would never have actually killed him, but looking back I can see the power of the belief that divorce was not an option for me. It kept me from taking action for a long time.

Maybe we feel helpless to act, never having had a model for having choices or possibilities.

Maybe we don't feel worthy of taking action on our own behalf.

We know that people who are raised in abusive situations learn to associate love with abuse. So they unconsciously recreate what has been familiar, even if it didn't feel good, because they thought that is what love was like.

Why would any of us ever stay in a belief system that doesn't feel good? We might even ask this question more universally— the behavior our entire human race is constantly distorted by unconscious beliefs about "the way it is supposed to be."

I mean really, if we actually thought deeply about it, why would people choose war as a way to solve a problem?

Why would we pollute our air and water?
Why would we stay in a boring soul-killing job or relationship?
Why do we put up with so much pain?

The answer can only be that we don't know that is it possible to change. And we don't know that we deserve the best.

I suspect that all of our (often unconscious) beliefs, actions, positioning, emotions, etc. are in place as distortions and smokes-creens to obscure this knowledge, even—or maybe especially—from ourselves. We do this for all kinds of reasons, I think, but they all add up to not feeling able to be who we really are in the world safely.

It would appear that all of the energy that goes into maintaining the contortions that keep unworthiness in place, in reality, has the positive intention of protecting us, even to the point of killing us. I have worked with so many people who, when they really looked deeply into a limiting belief or behavior, found an intention to secure peace, beauty, lightness, love, "heaven," in other words.

But the part of them that was trying to get all this goodness had very ineffective strategies, probably put in place long ago—and certainly picked up on the way into their incarnation from ancestral family energy patterns, that were in fact even damaging. Those parts just kept on running the same old patterns with the same old desperation, and getting the same old results without realizing it. Tunnel vision.

 I often think of a woman I used to work with, who was a victim of virtually lifelong sexual and emotional abuse from her parents and later from her husband. She had a heart attack in her early forties.

When she recovered consciousness in the hospital, and discovered what had happened and that she was still alive, she was thrown into an even deeper depression. She assumed that even God had rejected her, that she wasn't good enough to be in heaven—and so was sent back.

But to me the devastation she felt was telling. It said to me that there was a part of her that felt unbearably wounded by this thought: her pain meant to me that there was a essential being-ness in her that DID NOT BELIEVE IT AND THOUGHT SHE WAS WORTH WAY MORE THAN THAT. Sorry for shouting! Important point!

What creates cages?

It starts from how we experience growing up in our families—the beliefs that are handed down in our family experiences. Invisibility is a theme in my family.

My mother is a very strong, bright, creative light-filled being. But she is aware of none of that. She never feels seen or heard, or that she exists as an active force in the world.

So I grew up enthralled in that same trance, thinking of myself as being invisible. Later on, when I was studying Neuro-Linguistic Programming, the experience of discovering that it wasn't that I was invisible to other people, it was that I was invisible to myself, had a deep impact on me, and changed my view of myself completely.

After a long conversation with my mother recently, I woke up in the middle of the night trying to think of a way of describing my mother for her home health care coordinator. I was finding it hard to explain how my mother is not just the fuzzy-minded and sometimes-sweet but often stubborn and cranky old lady with dementia that she appears to be.

The image came to me of a Queen without a crown, a queen without a realm. I began thinking of other images that had the same sense of strong Presence, but Presence made invisible or obstructed. An opera singer without a voice. A wizard without a staff. I had a sense of the very intention of her life force having only a narrow, blocked channel to flow through.

My mother has the aspect to me of someone who has great power, awareness and wisdom, and a gracious heart, but who has seldom been able to exercise these capacities, or known how to use them, or even had the assurance that they were there at all. She was dominated, growing up, by two older brothers who she, and obviously her parents, idolized and favored.

Over the years her vitality and power has constricted into what

Profoundly light-hearted strategies for unsticking stuck stuff

manifests now as extreme passive aggressiveness, a highly critical demeanor—funnily enough she is most critical of people who are critical—and a victim mentality.

Her refrain in her life is always, "nobody sees me; nobody hears me; nobody lets me finish when I try to say something." She always feels herself to be the victim of another person's wishes (even when she is making them up, as she does increasingly, now). That makes her angry.

But—she *also* has an unconscious belief that she cannot express her anger, she cannot speak up for herself, and if she does no one will hear her anyway, and besides, no one understands. A psychologist would call this a passive-aggressive temperament.

We all have limiting beliefs that imprison us, encage us.

```
   > V  °   i°  °`^V  i°>  °i«i iV i°
 >  ° i`°  °>°L i iv°  >  ° >^°   i`°  ]°  °
   > i° i   }°>°L>  °v°  i°V > }i
```

The wonderful value of EFT, and of all the energy psychology techniques, is that each of them is good at removing bars of the cage. Until soon, there is space for you to step out of the cage!
And there you are, in your essential radiant sacred being-ness, visible to yourself, ready for presentation to the world in your own inimitable way!

I'm sure my mother got the "I'm invisible" belief from her parents who got it from their parents…back and back and back. My sister has her own version of it. I hope my daughters will have less of that invisibility issue to struggle through. Raising them, my strong intention was to mirror their strengths and abilities and beauty and power and essence back to them all the time.

Many good examples of the misaligned family beliefs that we are raised in come from our traditional religions. This is not a rant about religion, but an acknowledgment that in some of them we can find a source for our old beliefs about our low self worth, our sinfulness, our impure thoughts: turn the other cheek; always forgive; think of the other person first.

We also have beliefs about how hard and dangerous life is: It's a dog-eat-dog world; you're doomed from the start. Or, don't tell anyone anything—they'll have power over you if they know about you. Many people don't recognize that it's unusual, weird, or even damaging to have those beliefs.
There is the category of "hurry up", which is another way of saying, what you're doing is not important. Do it faster; do it better; do it quicker. What I need to have done is way more important than whatever you are doing.

And be strong! This is particularly endemic among people with chronic conditions. Tough it out. Soldier on. Hunker down. I can get through this—I've heard this so many times in the work I've done with people with fibromyalgia. I just have to get through this. I can take it. I can do this.

Or: you're not really sick.
You don't really feel that.
It didn't hurt that badly.
Another one you may hear is, "You don't look sick."

And it's true, people with chronic pain often present as being really together, well dressed, everything in place, usually very organized, very put together, having it all together.

Some Spirit-Shrinking Family Beliefs

SOLDIER BELIEFS
I have to tough it out
...hunker down
...soldier on

I must suffer what comes
Take it on the chin
I can take it
I just have to get through this and then things will be better

VICTIM BELIEFS

No one listens to me
I'm not good enough
I am not seen

SELF WORTH BELIEFS

I'll never be as good as _____
I am not smart enough
This is just the way I am/just the way it is
I have to do it perfectly (and I can't)

"BE PERFECT" BELIEFS

Death is better than making the wrong decision
We don't talk about unpleasant things
Don't get mad, get even
What will people think?

"TRY HARDER" BELIEFS

What you are doing is not good enough

"PLEASE ME, TAKE CARE OF ME" BELIEFS

Your needs are less important

"HURRY UP" BELIEFS

What you are doing is not important

"BE STRONG" BELIEFS

Big boys don't cry
Oh, Come on, that didn't really hurt.

What are some beliefs that you picked up from YOUR family that have held you back?

One person, reading these beliefs, wrote this to me:

I went to visit my sister and we went to her mother-in-law's house. On the wall in the kitchen was a plaque that read "Jesus First/Others Next/Yourself Last."

The first letter of each word was a different style and color and when you read them down it spelled, "JOY."

It made me so mad I wanted to scream, but I couldn't figure out why. I've since figured it out, of course, but I was so lost at that point in my life that I couldn't even see the reason for the anger.

Here is an exercise to find some of your own limiting beliefs and their effects. You can do this one as many times as you like. Tap for all of the thoughts, beliefs and feelings that come in response.

What Broke Your Heart?

Finish the sentences:
It broke my heart when....

What capacity did you feel was lost, broken or violated by those experiences?
I lost…

Profoundly light-hearted strategies for unsticking stuck stuff

Example:
connection
belonging
being visible
being heard
feeling
or being safe
worth,
deserving
inner power
self expression
etc…
Because of this I came to believe that….

I asked some of the people with chronic emotional and physical pain with whom I have worked to talk about their family's beliefs, the experiences that seemed to invoke those beliefs, and what they felt they had lost as a result. I have put some of the beliefs in bold. Look for others. Many are not stated, but implied.

NORMAN

The world is a dangerous place. My parents didn't say that, but neither parent was adept at negotiating daily life or street life, the life of getting what you wanted, being aggressive in the world. Though my mother was strong and insistent about what really mattered to her. Mother worried a lot, Father was kind of fearful.

It was important to be good, kind, loving. I rebelled against this; it was difficult. It was hard to be a boy and be that way at the same time. I was given so many messages about being so kind and loving that I couldn't believe it. **I knew I wasn't good in my heart. I lied and stole.**

We had a belief that **we were smart.** However, a strong belief that I have is a desire to **give up, to say "That is too hard."** People in my family were underachievers compared to a lot of other people. It seemed to me that adult life did not look that great. I was always striving to remain a boy, stay playful, avoid taking on responsibilities. My father settled into a job that didn't take much effort. It was low key. There was no appeal to studying in school. There was not a lot of pressure to succeed in my family. Things were disorganized. My mother's father was an unhappy person, sad, quite reserved. Mother did not want to be like him. Her parents had fought, and she did not want us to fight. There was a strong injunction against fighting. But we fought every day, all day. My parents never fought. It would have been useful if they had. Such an unruffled surface, the pleasantry between them.

Later, looking back, I think my mother was really unhappy with my father. She wanted more from him, more support, presence, to be more powerful, take a bigger role in the family. There was a fierceness about her that you didn't get to see that often. Some thwarted part of her. She wanted more.

There have been some incidents of panic in my life, and I became ill afterwards.

One was a car accident at 16. I didn't get injured but the car flipped over a guardrail at 60 miles an hour. Even a month later I was still believing **I was going to die in a car accident.** So much tension built up in my body. I said to my parents, "I am sure we are going to die in a wreck!" When we got home I went to bed. I said, **"I can't do this anymore."** I woke up and I was sick. It felt like the flu. I said "I can't go to school." I was sick for 10 days.

I sort of became ill to accommodate **the intolerable situation of being alive.**

THE 8 MASTER KEYS TO HEALING WHAT HURTS

Slowly I returned to normal, but after that each time something happened that frightened me I would become physically ill afterwards. If something happened that was traumatic, the fear would linger in my body and I would feel sick for days.

I was nervous about sex. When I was 17, I was getting involved with my girlfriend. She was very sweet. I became ill from the stress or trauma. My body had frozen up. There was a lot of fear that I didn't admit or express that I held inside. That is why I got sick.

Had I been able to be overt and loud and make a big deal about being afraid, admit it to myself and to the world, I would not have gotten sick.

That happened to the nth degree during an LSD trip when I was 18. I had been beaten up by a gang of teens because I had long hair.

I was fearful in general. I did not intend to be tripping on LSD this night, because I thought I had ingested a miniscule amount. I was harassed by the police, and I also thought my girlfriend was leaving me. Fear built up in me to at some point to become this physical thing, a rush of heat moving through me.

At that moment everything turned bad. Every thought became a physical sensation that was agonizing and painful. It felt as if this was permanent. Just like being in hell. It didn't easily go away after the LSD wore off. That experience changed me.

Makes me think of when people talk about stress from war, something stays in your body. You become jumpy, paranoid.

So to me, looking back, that incident led to becoming ill about a year after that. It was fairly similar to the illness I have had now for 36 years. Nancy Selfridge told me I had "fibromyalgia, or something like it."
At the time I was diagnosed with mono and hepatitis. I had extreme exhaustion, dragging around, couldn't get out of bed, tried to exert myself, tried to push through. I would get terrible headaches, my

Profoundly light-hearted strategies for unsticking stuck stuff

body would tighten up, I didn't feel like myself anymore. I felt like I had been taken over by some other being. I kept waiting to get well so I could be myself again. But that never happened. It has been 36 years now.

What the trip did was made me realize **how vulnerable I was.** It made me understand how fear could take you over. How terrible it could be. It left me **fearful of other people and situations.** I kept being fearful but still functioning. Maybe because I was a strong healthy young person, it was a while before I got worn down by that stress.

That was the most dramatic single incident. But it was preceded by all those experiences of being humiliated, hurting and being hurt in childhood, that created the desire to not be seen as vulnerable. But I felt vulnerable nonetheless.

MOIRA

From my mother I got the constant worry about "what did I accomplish today?" My father's side: **"prepare for the worst prepare for the worst prepare for the worst."**

There was no "expect the best."

My father was not a pessimist, he was delightful to be around in a lot of ways. But when I really looked at it, I saw no belief in a sustaining safe pattern or meaning behind everything. From my current vantage point it looks to me as if I was an extremely sensitive child and I didn't get the kind of safety, intimacy, quiet encouragement that I needed, so I tried to soldier on.

I was always trying to be a good girl, to prevail. My mom always said, "My life didn't make any sense until I met your dad. He gave my life coherency." Probably they both were sensitive types. This constant noisy bath of kids was tough, but it didn't feel to them like "meaningless chaos without spirit to it," like it did to me.

I came away from my family with a belief that **"I am a bossy, unpleasant person, smart, talented, but not lovable."** Up until I got sick with fibromyalgia I lived my life at a very high volume. I turned the volume up on my own conduct because I felt so drowned out by my surroundings, in school, in my family.

I think that was the keynote belief that I took away from those childhood experiences—that I was bossy and not pleasant. All my interactions with my mother had that theme. I don't really remember my childhood. I can't point to one thing. I was not raped, I didn't go to war. But I look back and say, oh my gosh, the whole thing.

I said to my friend dealing with chronic fatigue who is in dire straits, "At least if you are an orphan in an orphanage, the people who are not being nice to you are not your parents. At least you can dream about having good parents."

Deepak Chopra says that when the people who are supposed to be your dear ones act abusive toward you, dismissive, you have no safe place.

I see now **I didn't ever feel safe**. It was not conscious. I didn't actually say to myself, "even if I walk through the valley of death ...I am the meanest son of a bitch ever..." I didn't mean it that way but I acted that way because I didn't feel safe.

It wasn't until I got into Al-Anon meetings that could I let go of the idea that it doesn't have to always be my way. I can let go and still be safe. Then I became more fun to be around, more self-aware.

My life went from a big huge beach ball—an attorney, public defender, busy practice—to collapsed into almost nothing. Now I go for days and days and days without contact. But I'm starting to feel again what it is like to be alive. The hard part is I can't really do very much without getting the symptoms back again.

I didn't know that in my life I was being outwardly different from who I was on the inside.

STEPHANIE

The main belief in my family was **"It would be better to die than to have regret."** That is, you could make the wrong decision and it didn't turn out well and that was worse than death. Being wrong. I got the perfectionism from my dad. Being asked to clean up the kitchen—then he would look at it and say, "If you had done this and this, then it would have been perfect."

The effect of that in me was that I learned to **question every decision** from every which way and angle to make sure that I didn't make a bad decision. My mother—I remember the day I called them to say I was getting a divorce—She said "Are you sure? **It's really hard for a divorced woman to find another man."** You can see what her beliefs were.

It was really hard for me to develop my own perspective and believe in that and be sure of it. I would say to myself, "It's really hot out here -- but others are feeling chilly so **I must be wrong."**

I am always looking at everyone else from my mother's perspective that **my own idea isn't necessarily right.** There could be a positive effect of that. In work, for example, I can see both sides. But it makes you less confident and sound in who you are.

How can I know *what* I believe?

One of the major effects on me of my family's belief system is that I am constantly trying to avoid getting my feelings hurt and avoid the whole freeze situation. Over the years as those potentially dangerous and hurtful situations come up I have learned from them too well. I spend all my waking hours and energy on constantly trying to plan my way out of getting in those situations again. The cage gets smaller.

I remember in 6th grade we were all lined up go back in after playground, and the girl who had been my best friend, but also the queen bee, decided that she didn't like me after all, and she proceeded to tell me how much she hated me in front of all the other kids. That kind of queen bee person recognizes the sensitive ones and uses them as a target. It was me and her and a third girl, and I was always the one on the outside. That experience was a trauma for me. It shocked me.

There was another similar imprint in junior high. The 8th graders had a tradition of mentoring the 7th graders. I had a party in 7th grade early in the school year just for 7th graders. Later at the football stadium, a lofty 8th grader dressed me up and down in front of everyone for "hating 8th graders."

This was an example of how I always feel now that **there are all these unwritten rules, which other people seem to know about but I don't**. My life has become about always trying to see them before I trip over them.

That's the whole thing about unwritten rules—you can't see them until you break them. And then it is too late. All my obsessive planning and thinking and trying to figure it all out never works. It just made me sick.

When your parents call you a cry-baby, that is not a good feeling. I got spanked a lot when I was little. At the time it was a common way of raising children, though I wasn't a rebellious kid. But I was so sensitive, they really only had to look at me cross-eyed.

One day things were going really well, and I was noticing that, and then I got spanked later in day for something I didn't know was bad. I have that as a belief now. **Just when things go well, something bad happens**. It is a belief in **being unsafe**, never knowing when things will blow up.

Along the same lines, when I look at my father now I think he had sensitivity. He had a very big startle reflex, hair trigger temper. He would startle first, and then be mad. It was always very scary for me.

GINA

I was called the black sheep from the time I remember. I'm not sure why. That's what my mother was called in her family too. My brothers were gods—**I could never be as good as them.** I must have been mischievous, maybe into everything. I was really curious. But no one took the time to do anything creative with me.

I came away from my childhood with a belief: **"Why bother starting anything—you never finish it."** I was told that "The only reason women go to college is to get their Mrs. It is a waste of money – they just get married and have babies anyway." Speak when spoken to. **Children are to be seen, not heard. My opinions weren't relevant or important.**

I was rebellious. Told that from the time I was a kid. Later on I found out my mother and father used to be partiers; my mother even rode a motorcycle.

As a child I would do things I wasn't "supposed" to do. Making mud pies, typical kid stuff. My mother didn't like dirty. As a teen I was the one who snuck out to meet my boyfriend, drank alcohol, took drugs, had sex at 15. My mother never said a thing. I made a pathetic attempt at suicide at 15—cut my wrists. All my mother said afterwards was, "Are you pregnant?" She never knew I was really unhappy. But I didn't really want to die. My father never learned of it, and never said anything to me.

In my early 20's I made another suicide attempt. I was really saying that I was in trouble, I needed help. I would have benefited from therapy, someone to talk to. All my mother said was that, "we are not going to tell Dad." She never got it, never asked how I was doing. My mother was an ostrich. Anything she didn't want to deal with, she didn't look at. My Dad was never around.

Since I never had any encouragement, I never pursued making anything of myself. As I got older I didn't go to college; I started working full time, I never gave any thought to having a career. I believed my mother—women are to get married and have babies. Work was so unfulfilling and I seemed less and less likely to have babies.

There was a lot of emotional neglect. My parents believed their role was to provide food, clothes, roof. That was the extent of parenting. You didn't show affection, say, "I love you." They thought **you'd spoil kids if you tell them you love them too often**. I didn't have any support system as a child.

There were some good beliefs in my family.

But—they were said but not lived by.

ALL THE TRUE VOWS

All the true vows
are secret vows
the ones we speak out loud
are the ones we break.

There is only one life
you can call your own
and a thousand others
you can call by any name you want.

Hold to the truth you make
every day with your own body,
don't turn your face away.

Hold to your own truth
at the center of the image
you were born with.

Those who do not understand
their destiny will never understand
the friends they have made
nor the work they have chosen

nor the one life that waits
beyond all the others.

By the lake in the wood
in the shadows
you can
whisper that truth
to the quiet reflection
you see in the water.

THE 8 MASTER KEYS TO HEALING WHAT HURTS

Whatever you hear from
the water, remember,

it wants to carry
the sound of its truth on your lips.

Remember,
in this place
no one can hear you

and out of the silence
you can make a promise
it will kill you to break,

that way you'll find
what is real and what is not.

I know what I am saying.
Time almost forsook me
and I looked again.

Seeing my reflection
I broke a promise
and spoke
for the first time
after all these years

in my own voice,

before it was too late
to turn my face again

David Whyte
The House of Belonging

❀❀ ❀ ❀ ❀ ❀

8
THE PHYSIOLOGY OF NEGATIVE BELIEFS

WHAT HAPPENS IN YOUR BODY WHEN YOU ARE MAD, SAD, OR SCARED?

(Refer to the Master Key Map in the Discovery Book)

Experiences Lead to Beliefs...
Lead to Feelings…
…Can Lead to Illness and Pain

When that painful experience happens to you, and you begin to take on a negative belief about yourself, or about what is possible for you in the world, how does that make you feel?

What happens in your body as a result?

How do you find yourself acting?

4 – Response:
How does that belief make you feel?

Think of the first time/worst time/or a vivid example in your life of when you felt this emotion.

Ask yourself:

What effects has it had in your life?
How does it make you act?
If you could find that emotion in your body, where would it be?
What physical symptoms are associated with it?

❊ ❊ ❊

4 – Response:
Where do you feel pain?

Notice how it feels in your body. Describe it.

Ask yourself:

If there were an emotion behind this or connected to this, what would it be?

What does this emotion remind me of? What experience in the past? Especially as a child…

❊ ❊ ❊

THE FORMULA:

Repeated experiences of stress or trauma can cause…

❊ The energy system to become disrupted -
❊ The flow of life force restricted -
❊ Limited access to our capacity…
❊ Limited ability to think and act and make choices.

IDENTITY

I came to believe _____ about myself
(I can't be or do anything. I will mess it up.
Nothing I do is enough or good enough.
Cloudy thinking; depression)

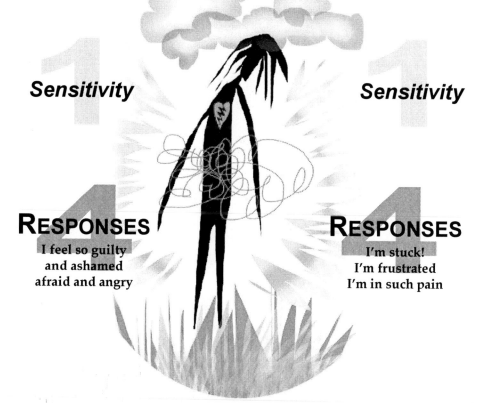

Sensitivity

Sensitivity

RESPONSES

I feel so guilty
and ashamed
afraid and angry

RESPONSES

I'm stuck!
I'm frustrated
I'm in such pain

PAIN-ful Experience

(Title: I'm Overwhelmed and Engulfed by My Mother's Rage)

```
         °      ° v °V    V °« >      °
      > ^ °> ° \ ^ >    ° v ° i°^«      ° °
```

There are descriptions of fibromyalgia in traditional Chinese medicine which use the phrase "vexation of the spirit." I like that very evocative term.

This disharmony of spirit is reflected as pain in the body when we restrict the expression of our deepest truth in our lives, whatever that truth is.

```
 ,i^  V  }°  > i i° > i^° ^°    i ° ^p  °
   v ii }° ° i^ V i'p i^ ^° °> }i]°v i> ]°
       ^> ' i^^]°^ > i]°> \°    >    ° °
```

It all seems to come down to this statement that somebody with fibro or chronic pain might feel unconsciously but not be able to articulate, or even be aware of:

"I can't express what I really feel. In order to get a sense that I have control over what happens to me, and in order to justify taking care of *myself*—instead of the rest of the world—I must remain ill."

```
        °L i i i°  > °V    V °« >  ° ^ °>
   `i« i^^  ]°L^ V  ]°  ° i «   ° °> °
      « > V > °^i^  i°«i^ ‰ ^°
            i i }°^ ^ i
```

SOME ENERGY PSYCHOLOGY

All the experiences we had as children have led us to create certain beliefs about who we are and how much we deserve to be here, and what is possible. But the process starts even earlier—before we are even born.

We are born into a family story about "the way it is supposed to be." So even in the womb, we are literally surrounded by and absorb the effects of our mother's family story in its effects on her body, mind, emotions and spirit at the cellular level of her body, our host. We feel the effects of our father's family story in our DNA, energetically, and in our mother's responses to him, even before our birth.

This story seems to get repeated down generation after generation. How does that happen?

And even scientists are learning to trust their intuition!

Candace Pert, the neuro-scientist who discovered that neuro-transmitters flow throughout the whole body, not just in the brain, and who was featured in the film *"What the Bleep do We Know,"* says that she is beginning to operate on the "you're getting warmer; you're getting colder" rule of thumb.

I love those words coming from a scientist! So, the following account feels like getting warmer.

I came across this description from the writings of an accomplished and respected practitioner of Traditional Chinese medicine. It offers a wonderful lyrical explanation for this interesting question. I call it lyrical because this explanation is not yet fully proven scientifically, or medically accepted, but it feels true.

In traditional Chinese medicine, the heart houses the body's spirit. "Shen" is the Chinese name for the body's spirit.

THE 8 MASTER KEYS TO HEALING WHAT HURTS

The heart actually generates 40-60 times more electromagnetic charge than any other system in the body, including the brain.

Negative experiences create a disharmony in the energy system and displace the mind-body-spirit alignment.   This is the energy disruption "zzzzt" that Gary Craig talks about in the Basic Recipe manual for EFT.

Here is William Lieske, an acupuncturist and respected doctor of Traditional Chinese Medicine, with a description of this process.

He begins by saying that the very first beat of the heart in a fetus in the womb begins our path as a human life.

And he continues:

"…The second beat, and the first in what will determine our identity, is the amygdala. The amygdala starts forming immediately after the heart's first beat. It stores all the memories of our life in the womb, with the placenta, the water, the fluids of life and the terror of losing them, and also the joy of being fed, of bouncing, of moving. But the amygdala stores also the life of the mother, her depressions, her fears, her life. And this accumulation of memories goes on in us till the age of three. Which means that all this time we have lived, our life has been recorded for us in the amydgala.

"After the age of three the hippocampus matures in us. In it conscious memories are stored and we have access to them. However, in the hippocampus, we have no access to the memories and the life we lived in the amygdala of the previous three years, even if from this point on amygdala and hippocampus converse with each other (Carter, Rita, 1998).

"What happens to the memories of the amygdala? They become our individual nightmare, the invisible conditioning of all our actions, the blind spot of our lives, the origin of all our terrors, the unknown reason why we do what we done even when we do not know why we do it....

"The conditioning of the amygdala can only be removed by the intelligence system previous to it, and this is the heart, with its electromagnetic force and its power of transformation. Otherwise, the amygdala can act on its own, bypassing the intelligence centers of the neocortex. [Our limiting beliefs] keep acting, in spite of our good intentions."

Lieske.com/channels.htm

VIP: vaso-active intestinal peptide

Some of the newest developments in science add to this image. It is actually scientifically known that the fetus does not have the capacity to create its own VIP, but it is loaded with receptors for VIP.

VIP, as Candace Pert and others have discovered, is *vaso-active intestinal peptide.*

The prevailing emotion associated with high levels of VIP is high sense of self-esteem. So the fetus has abundant receptors and no ability to create VIP on its own. All of that receptor–triggering comes from the mother's VIP number.

Vaso-active intestinal peptide does a lot of things in the body, but the emotional tone that it creates is associated with a high sense of self-esteem. The developing fetus has abundant receptors for VIP and no capacity to create the substance on its own. It's completely reliant on Mother to create that.

Choose your mother wisely! Because, if mother has a low sense of self-esteem, what the amygdala is picking up as the fetus is growing is all the fear stuff, the alarm stuff, the negative self worth stuff.

The amygdala continues to record experience up through the age of three. Between ages three and seven there is also an open window for the recording of experience, and especially what it *means*—the beliefs—as well.

All of these patterns—the family belief system, our family pattern of ways of thinking and functioning in the world—lie waiting within us at the unconscious level.

When we encounter a negative experience that resonates with an existing pattern, it is awakened in us, and sets that pattern off to reverberate in our lives.

We grow up with those patterns still in place. They act like a magnet, an energy field that draws to us the kinds of daily experiences that will trigger the stuck responses.

The experiences we have as children activate the energy patterns of the constricted beliefs that are already set in place within us. That is what cages the expression of our deepest humanity. I believe that this is what we think of as genetic inheritance. Again, I don't know if this is scientifically true in the Western sense, but it is true according to Traditional Chinese Medicine, and it FEELS true.

EFT, TAT (Tapas Acupressure Treatment), and all other Energy Psychology techniques affect the body's energy system, restoring the alignment between the mind-body-spirit. They open the cage and restore our capacity to make choices. They help disconnect the stuck stuff.

❋ ❋ ❋ ❋ ❋

Checking in with folks again...

LEILA

Here are portions of an email conversation I had with Leila, the woman with fibromyalgia who you met in Chapter 6, on Painful Experiences. This conversation followed our very first telephone conversation, though we had a number of email conversations prior to this session. I had introduced her to EFT through email, and she had been tapping on her own with input from me for a few months, with very good results.

Dear Rue, Thank you so much for our phone call yesterday. I've barely had a chance to think about it because right after talking to you, I had to make a car trip out of town, which has knocked me for a loop now. It was a rough day yesterday—my nervous system hasn't been tested like that for a long time, and though I'm sure I coped better than in the past, my brain and body are overwhelmed. It would have been better if I'd had a chance to think about our conversation.

I can remember parts of it though - especially trying to learn to say thank you if someone compliments me, instead of cringing in cynical disbelief. Also, that part of the conclusion was that I need to tap (probably a lot and for some time persistently) on disconnecting my present day reactions from those instilled in me by my mother's very negative input and those instilled in me by abusive men who used violence to frighten me into obedience (a continuation of how I was treated as a very young child).

I want to learn to grow my stronger side and learn to disconnect from the part of me that is so easily frightened and cowed into a subservient, submissive posture. I have to honor that little girl who was unable to stand up to the dominance and beatings of my baby self, and honor the adult woman who also caved in under threats and physical violence and enormous fear. I have felt weak and ashamed for so many years—it's hard to make the shift to positive and proud.

The best shift that happened while I was talking to you came when you were able to coax me to say out loud, "I am of value" and then even, "I am of great value." !! I was surprised by how sure of that I was—the sureness came from deep inside—and I am certain that it is a result of the EFT work I have done over the last few months—especially gently rubbing over my heart and saying, "I deeply and completely love and except myself." What a gift this is. I can feel God teaching us all about love. How lucky we are.

Do you have any ideas of a tapping sequence to help me release my mom's damage to me? I can use your visualization of a tree with the patterns of damage caught in the branches (thinking) and roots (past), and fit in, "mom's damage to me," and then release all the negative emotions connected to that one at a time, and persistently.

Thank you so much for being there and all your wonderful gentle help. I like your voice so much—it reminds me of the spirits in the woods. My old friend Nell (who died a few years ago) had an unswerving belief in the fairies and saw them everywhere—lightening and sparkling everything. That's how I felt after talking to you. Next time, hopefully I won't have a long road trip on the same day, or if I do I'll be able to handle it—no problem!!

In a reply to her I pointed out the "Freudian slip" of "I love and except myself". How appropriate a mistake for someone who has thought she has no value!

Rage

More memories of our conversation have come back to me now. It reminds me of trying to pick up loose mercury after a thermometer breaks (remember those old thermometers?). My poor memory recall is getting a little alarming—but it's OK—this bits and pieces recall method works too!

More importantly—I have realized how much stronger my anger is towards my mother over awful things she did to others than it is over anything she did to me. You gently pushed me a bit to recall those feelings and I came up with almost nothing—but huge rage over her treatment of others.

Today I thought my way through to understanding that from a very young age I knew two things from my DAD! That I was a disappointment and that young 'soldiers' have to toughen up. So two things developed in me at the same time—an acceptance that I deserved to be thought poorly of and a toughness to carry pain and 'keep my chin up" and not fight back against the commander—mom.

My Dad's war experience cut him off from his own sensitivities and he saw his children's frailties as weaknesses. So now I understand better why I have trouble recalling my buried anger directly related to mom's treatment of ME.

I thought I deserved it and that I had to learn to be tough. It wasn't until I was a teenager that I began to feel anger—but even that was mainly about mom's treatment of others.

So the origins of my low self-esteem (and the fibromyalgia) are buried very very deep. Whatever anger I may have felt and buried as a very young child was pushed down even further by the certainty that I was a bad girl and deserved (more than the other children) to be treated poorly—and that my ability to accept that treatment meant I was becoming a good little soldier.

No wonder I have trouble recalling anger over how I was treated, but no trouble recalling anger over how the rest of my family was treated.

That was so interesting to me, just how blank I was when you asked me to specifically recall my own personal anger over how I was treated. I'm onto it now though, and will work on getting some tappable phrases figured out. Thank you Thank you!

Dad's involvement...

Obviously writing the above emails sparked her thinking, because a day later this email came:

...However, this fibromyalgia is dug in deep. Talking to you last Wednesday really helped me uncover a whole new aspect, when I realized that the enormous anger I carry towards my mother is mainly related to her mistreatment of OTHERS. The anger I carry about her mistreatment of ME is buried much much deeper.

So why, why, why is that?? And ah - hah! I have finally uncovered my father's involvement!!

By the way, I do fully understand that they were doing the best they could with what they had (their own wounded selves) and the damage they did was completely unintentional—just like me—and look at the unintentional damage I did!!!!!

Yes, the lights are finally coming on here!!

So, for fibromyalgia, it feels necessary to do the 'hard work in the trenches' even after having these mental breakthroughs. Do you find that to be generally true?

Here are what I found to be tappable phrases about my father's involvement in my ability to stuff my anger way down deep into potential fibromyalgia territory. I haven't tapped on them yet, but when I do I'll let you know how it goes. I am so looking forward to breaking out of all this into the light—
I know I'm already well on my way.

So, the hard work part:

Even though—(each of the below)—I deeply and completely love and accept myself and am open to healing the situation now.

...my dad treated me like I was a disappointment

...my dad treated me like a young soldier who had to toughen up

...my dad taught me to accept that I deserved to be thought poorly of

...my dad taught me how to be tough

...my dad taught me to keep my chin up and carry the emotional and physical pain

...my dad taught me not to fight back against mom

...my dad saw his children's frailties as weaknesses

...my dad's war experience cut him off from his own sensitivities

...I have trouble recalling my buried anger directly related to mom's treatment of ME

...I thought I deserved it and I had to be tough

...the anger I felt was pushed very far down inside

...the origins of the low self esteem are buried very deep

...the anger was pushed down by the certainty that I was a bad girl

...the anger was pushed down by the certainty that I deserved to be treated badly

...my ability to accept that treatment meant I was becoming a good little soldier, which won dad's silent approval

Time to get to work on this.

Love, and thank you so much, Leila

GINA

My brother is married to a woman with two exceptionally talented daughters. My older sister had a beautiful voice. I was invited to her performance to hear her sing. She was amazing. My brother was going on and on and on about her. I thought, "If I don't get out of this room I am going to start screaming!" I had to leave. I was thinking, "Why in hell did you never encourage me? Never recognize me?" No one in my family encouraged me to do anything. I can sing too!

My brothers were the gods in my family. They got everything!

I felt such anger and grief. I was in tears all the way home. This should have been me! Like I'm getting my nose rubbed in this. I will never again be able to go out and see her sing. Or see anyone in my family getting recognition.

When I kept a list of all the things I was angry about, to tap on, my anger list was very long.

And then I am angry at myself for being angry!

I finally quit my job last year because I was angry at my boss ALL the time. It put my family in a terrible financial situation. If she hadn't been such a horrible manager I could have put up with the job. I wrote a scathing letter to her. I felt better for awhile. Of course I never mailed it.

I have anger at myself for not having figured out how to let go of my anger. I am sad that I am sad. I have to be careful, thinking I have no right to be angry and sad any more. Now I feel guilty if I am not happy and blissful that I am not in that job. I feel like I have to be up and happy and chipper for my husband.

It made me angry that I couldn't tough it out. I should be able to do this job. Not being able to tough it out would be a failure in my family, a sign of weakness. I should be able to let it roll off, not let it bother me. That is a philosophy I I was raised with. If you got hurt: "Oh you're not that bad, just tough it out." I didn't tell my dad I had quit my job because he would see me as a failure.

Now after the work we have done, and all the tapping, I knew in my heart that the failure would have been to stay in that job.

THE 8 MASTER KEYS TO HEALING WHAT HURTS

One of the hardest things about this healing work is that it really is hard work. It is asking people to REALLY look at their injuries and wounds. You feel that pain again.

I found the tapping could let me get rid of anger if I could focus on what it was the tapping helped me get rid of. Then I could let go of the anger.

I can't explain it. It just makes you feel better.

Getting rid of anger, I feel more relaxed. I hold anger tension in my body as a coiled spring.

I can literally feel tenseness draining out of me and I can breathe and relax.

The other thing that tapping really does for me is that phrase, "even though...I deeply and completely love and accept myself" has had a profound effect on my own sense of value. I have come to appreciate myself, recognize myself, my own intelligence.

EFT gets that phrase into your belief system. It gets into your cells somehow.

I think I always knew I was intelligent but didn't want anyone to know. I wasn't capable of acknowledging that because that is being proud, conceited. "You don't toot your own horn." "Don't break your arm patting yourself on the back." "If I don't do it no one else will." My parents grew up with those impoverished beliefs.

My grandmother told me she regretted that she did not show more affection and encouragement to her children. She thought they would be spoiled. She saw her son doing the same thing to his kids. She told my dad that she was born out of wedlock. Her mother (this is my great-grandmother) then married a man they found for her who was "willing to take her as damaged goods." This husband

Profoundly light-hearted strategies for unsticking stuck stuff

verbally abused her. So I can see how it gets passed down through the generations.

MOIRA

I was working at the public defender's office as a lawyer, had been in law for 8 years. Working really really hard without stopping. And before that I had worked hard. I started getting sick but I didn't pay attention, I thought it would go away. I felt dizzy and sick, flu-ish, malaise. I was getting sicker and sicker.

As I had for years I went to work. If you didn't go to work your caseload was like a train wreck. It got to the point where I couldn't think straight. I remember sitting in rooms in the courthouse saying to myself, "I can't think straight, I don't know if this is a good deal."

Six weeks later, I went to the doctor. He said I had to go home. I slept for 30 days almost around clock. I tried to go back to work. Went back 1-2 hrs a day—it was like trying to go to work when you are at the height of the flu, so sick you can't get dressed.

I couldn't fathom being this sick and living through it. It went on for months and months.

The first diagnosis was chronic fatigue, but I wouldn't accept the diagnosis because I read that with CF you couldn't get well. The doctor said OK. He knew this wasn't like me. I didn't have to convince someone I wasn't making this up.

My life sort of came to a stop. Now, if I am in a fraction of what used to be a normal day, now I have to just sit, or the symptoms come back. My life is structured around what I can do. As a result there is a lot of silence around me.

The solitude, I felt so unsafe even in solitude. That brought to my attention that I didn't feel safe inside myself and wasn't really present in myself. I didn't know how I felt at any time day or night.

I had lost the ability to know that I was
home in my body.

If I was with another person, that was experienced as a traumatic event. There was hitting in my family as a little kid. I realized that other people seemed dangerous to me. I did my best to present to people a facsimile of what I would be if I could actually be there.

When I am around people I won't necessarily be able to stay inside and stay in touch. I am not ready yet to be around people. That is a big deal for me, exhausting.

I have a lot of grief, terrible feelings of despair and loss and hopelessness. I can hardly bear to look at it. It is exactly like Post Traumatic Stress Disorder. If I would start thinking about it, then I would start reliving it. And then I would feel, "What's the use. There is no way out."

If I try to talk with my mom about how I feel, I get waves of pity from her—it is terrifying. It confirms my feeling that my situation is hopeless. You don't know there is another way, all that stuff you absorbed as a child, you think that is the way life is.

The feeling I get from my mom is that I am a baby from a litter that is deformed and not going to be OK, it is hopeless and so sad. This life that had so much promise, is a mangled hopeless sad thing. Makes me feel sick. In her life, "I was the runt of the litter," no one loved me. But I have to remind myself: "This is my mom, she does this. It doesn't mean anything about me—whether I am a useful or meaningful person with something to offer in world."

Since getting sick I have changed the way I operate so profoundly, and forgiven so much. And yet it is like I have this nasty angry part that seems to be almost as strong, as prevalent as when I started.

Just yesterday, I was feeling I have been robbed of my abilities to do what I am fitted for, the life I had intended to live, by my childhood and the way life is set up, by my nature.

Now, if I am alone long enough to settle in,
I am getting to the point where I know
how I feel.

I need a lot of solitude to settle into my body, feel alive. I can stay with myself and tell how I'm feeling. I walk my dog at night near the lake and it is so beautiful. I noticed that once the people are all gone, the atmosphere changes. Everything is very still and very present. I would cry. I would walk and cry every night.

Gradually I began to feel joy. Peace.

Now I am noticing when something feels a certain kind of beautiful, true, authentic, spiritual, touchstone inside. Positive.

MADELYN

Here is a list of what has showed up in me over time as symptoms: migraines, headaches, menstruation problems, face pain, pain in the muscles in my cheeks, my teeth hurt, my jaw hurt. Neck, arm, joints from lymph. There has been pain in my stomach, back, and butt. When I have been sitting too long, my legs and calves grip up on me. My feet used to hurt a lot, but that is not too bad now. I have had problems sleeping, irritable bowel syndrome, loss of libido. I have a very sensitive temperament and sensitive body.

I feel that my body is betraying me. It is not cooperating. There are things I want to do and it is not cooperating.

During college I decided that overachieving was fun. I thought if I worked harder I could get straight A's. Then I decided if I could take heavier course load and still get straight A's, it would be an even bigger achievement. Then I went on to finish my degree in 2 years, 9 mo. I graduated on the Dean's list. My senior year is when the migraines started.

> Achieving high results felt really good, but there is
> a piece that what I do is never good enough.

It goes back to the perfectionist thing.

In my family it was about never getting a lot of praise for doing well. The refrain was, "You can do better, you can do better." I am continuing to try to get that praise. Who am I trying to get it from now? Everyone I can. Trying to get it from myself.

My first symptoms seemed to be more a food-related trigger. Maybe it was actually from underlying stress. Normal work kind of charged me up but then things would start humming at a higher rpm. I would get Irritable Bowel Syndrome. I reacted to fried potatoes, high fat foods, mayo, cream-based soup.

The next ratchet up was work-incident stress. I was planning work inventories, there were pressures and expectations and demands, change, requests. It was very stressful. My hair was falling out in gobs. I was diagnosed with TMJ. Then I went to the chiropractor—he diagnosed it as back problems. The doctor diagnosed it as sinuses. Now I know it was fibromyalgia. Whatever muscles I last stressed got stuck.

> Whenever I was diagnosed by a specialist, they said I had
> whatever they treated.

The next ratchet up, I got a job that was very political, and it required me to travel a lot. There were long days, debating, late dinners, trying to sleep, my mind spinning, trying to reason out the arguments.

THE 8 MASTER KEYS TO HEALING WHAT HURTS

I ended up with more jaw pain, headache, pain in my back, more sleep problems.

I took a different job, and then I found a lump in my breast. It was breast cancer. I had chemo and radiation, and that took stress up to the next level.

I think the beliefs behind all these physical symptoms stem from perfectionism. In my 20's I had more balance, but now my cage feels like it is getting smaller; the balance is tipping the other way. I used to like to socialize, but I know from past experience that I will have pain. My world is getting smaller.

There is always this sense in me that there are unwritten rules that I don't know about.

That's hard—you lose your zest for life, your ability to take it in and enjoy it, just do it and not think about it. I always have to analyze-plan-reflect-figure. There is no spontaneity, no trust in my own instincts.

There is also not being revealing. I am not a very revealing person because I don't want to put myself out there, don't want to get hurt. But this way you end up not really fully being you, I think.

There is always a question - did I do something to bring this on? Could I have avoided it? Could I have planned my way around it so it wouldn't happen? In my family, if you made a mistake - someone would say, "I guess you should have thought of that."

I do that to myself all the time. "What is wrong with you that you didn't think of it?" I beat myself up but it's more tied into thinking that if I'd thought of it I wouldn't be in this hurtful situation. I didn't apply enough energy, didn't think enough. I do that kind of thinking 24 hours a day, even when I am supposed to be sleeping.

Your planning mechanism is in overdrive. The more pain and other

Profoundly light-hearted strategies for unsticking stuck stuff

symptoms, the more you have to plan in order to work around avoiding a spiral into an un-winnable situation. It is hopeless. My way is to plan, plan, plan, but I'm always one step behind.

Earlier in my life I was quite charged up about my life. Lately now it's negative. My analogy: those little merry go round things at the playground, where you push on the bars and run and hop up ride for awhile 'til it slows down. When it works like that it's fun. And if you ever were running and pushing it and losing your footing, you'd have to hop up onto it or fall down and hurt yourself.

I feel now like I am running and running and can't get my feet under me - but if I let go I will get hurt. If I can just run a little harder I can get my felt under me again. If I let go and roll - but I can't quite get myself to risk the pain. I am presuming that I can get my feet under me again. Do you think I am wrong?

SALLY

I have been doing a great deal of thinking about my life before the pain and how small and constricted my life became after the pain. I am feeling a great deal of grief about all that I have lost in those years of pain. And...

...I want my life back again!
I will heal.

I want to be hopeful, and I am hopeful much of the time, but the old fears come back and want to pull me down. I guess that is just the way this works.

I really need to work on my fear of the pain. It is taking all my attention. I can't think about much else. I'm sure I could also decrease my need for medication if I was not so absorbed in fretting

Profoundly light-hearted strategies for unsticking stuck stuff

and worrying about the pain. What is the best way to go about this?
Is there any special way I should tap for this?

This is probably a cluster of fears—fear of the pain itself, fear of how
bad the pain will get at any given time, fear of if and/or when the
pain will lessen, fear of how long the pain will last, fear of how long
I am going without exercise, fear of how this will impact my severe
osteoporosis.

That looks like a good bunch of fears to tackle.

THE LARGEST POSSIBLE LIFE

by Alison Luterman

for Ruth and Gladys

Building a fire, love;
   bent low
      over a flame

I am afraid of.
   Coaxing passion
      from dry twigs

and dead leaves,
   the failures of the past, dirty fingers,
      and a moment of sunset

huge orange
   hangs in one eye—
      in my breast a sun

which, if I could see it, if I could
   know it, would
      light the world

with love. Then,
   an unexpected memory
      of my mother in the car, snow piled

along the gray streets
   of Massachusetts. It was my sixteenth year
      and we were fighting a life

and death struggle over my desire to give
   myself away completely to love before
      I had a self to give.

There she was, my block, my barricade,
   my iron grate, my broken door-our one shared
      passion, to hurt each other into truth, and

it was the millionth skirmish
    of our everyday war when she said
        "I don't know if I've ever loved anyone,"

and began to weep. Monks sit
    in the middle of fires
        they set themselves. They let

their bodies bloom
    into suffering,
        in the hope that, like this, they will open

someone's heart.
    What do we have to
        see, how close do we need to live by the

beautiful terrible flame of this world,
    flame of ourselves, which is
        the same thing?

How much anguish do we need to pour
    from cup to cup, drink of melted rubies,
        underwater food of the fevers that live

in our blood, in the light of our eyes
    where infinite tears are waiting and still
        you say, "Light a white candle," and I do, asking

whoever it is, Teach me to surrender
    this mind that grasps at shadows
        when the whole house is ablaze, when the only thing left

is to leap, carrying the impossible
    weight in my arms, into
        the heart of our fire, to melt and to bloom.

from *The Largest Possible Life*,
Cleveland State Univ Poetry Center (March 30, 2001)
Reprinted with permission

❄ ❄ ❄ ❄ ❄

9
WHAT COULD BE POSITIVE?

INTENTION

When I feel pain, hurt or anger, my heart is trying to tell me that I deserve better! I've been caging my spirit and **I deserve better!**

5

Profoundly light-hearted strategies for unsticking stuck stuff

5 - Intention: What could be positive about this?

The best jumping-off points in creating the Map are your emotions or your physical symptoms.

Consider an apparently negative emotion, behavior, symptom, or belief, and then ask:

❄ What is the positive intention of that emotion/behavior/symptom?

❄ If the part of you that is running that behavior were trying to get something *for* you, what would it be?

❄ What could be good about this?

❄ What is a context in which this would be useful?

❄ Now, ask inside, if this part of you could have access to other, more powerful and much more effective strategies to get the safety/protection/love/attention it has been trying to get for you, would it be interested?

"Should I Keep the Pain...
...to Make Sure I Learn the Lesson it is Teaching Me?"

I did a telephone session with a woman who asked a wonderful question relating to healing chronic pain. She has had fibromyalgia for 20 years. This was our first session, and she was just beginning to explore EFT as a treatment modality. She had done a little on her own, but hadn't worked with anyone before using EFT in our session.

After I had gathered some information about her concerns, I asked what particular symptom or pain did she want to work with? She had a prior question she needed an answer to before we began.

Was there a chance, she asked, that EFT could be used as an aversion strategy?

"I believe that life is meant to be experienced," she said, seriously. "I don't want to take away the pain if that means I am just taking the easy way out. Is there a lesson for me here that I will miss if EFT takes away the pain? I want to evolve!

I don't want to foster the laziness in me. I don't want to not be proactive."

I found that very touching. Here she had been in pain for 20 years, and was *willing to continue* to be in pain if there was still something to be learned from it. Only someone really strong and determined could say that!

Or...someone who was "getting something" from enduring the pain.

How many of us believe that we must endure great hardship in order to evolve into our higher spiritual purpose? While I really honor her desire to learn and evolve, I think her strength and willingness to "take it in the name of growth" are seriously misguided.

I personally don't believe that we are meant to suffer *in order* to learn. I do believe that our suffering is meant to get our attention, and let us know that there is something awry, something flawed, something skewed in our personal belief system.

I do want to advance the heretical thought that we can learn just as easily, better, in fact, when we are relaxed and comfortable and looking forward to the possibilities instead of back toward all that we have not done perfectly. In my opinion, suffering seldom serves a higher purpose. I think that if it hurts, that is not good.

If this woman has been hurting for 20 years she is definitely not taking the easy way out! Her strength and resolve are being misdirected. Good intentions, bad direction.

But coming back to that point about getting something from enduring the pain. It reminds me of a story that I heard about the Japanese soldiers in World War II.

In their book, *The Heart of the Mind*, Connirae and Steve Andreas tell about the Japanese garrisons of soldiers who remained on thousands of tiny islands in the Pacific Ocean. Most of these garrisons were dismantled after the war, but there had been so many that some were entirely missed.

The soldiers on these islands often took to the caves, struggling to stay alive and true to the mission that they took on to protect and defend their motherland. They maintained their tattered uniforms and rusting weapons as best they could, longing to be reunited with their central command. Even thirty years after the war had ended, these few remaining soldiers were still being encountered by natives, tourists, fishing boats.

Consider the position of such a soldier. As the Andreas' say:

"His government had called him, trained him, and sent him off to a jungle island to defend and protect his people against great external threat. As a loyal and obedient citizen, he had survived many privations ad battles through the years of war. When the ebb and flow of battle passed him by, he was left alone or with a few other survivors. During all those years, he had carried on the battle in the best way he could, surviving against incredible odds. Despite the heat, the insects, and the jungle rains, he carried on, still loyal to the instructions given to him by his government so long ago."

They ask, "How should such a soldier be treated when he is found? It would be easy to ridicule him, or call him stupid to continue to fight a war that had been over for 30 years.

But the Japanese government, bless them, took a very different tack with these old soldiers. The Andreas' continue:

"Instead, whenever one of these soldiers was located, the first contact

Profoundly light-hearted strategies for unsticking stuck stuff

was always made very carefully. Someone who had bee a high ranking Japanese officer during the war would take his old uniform and samurai sword out of his closet, and take an old military boat to the area where the lost soldier had been sighted.

"The officer would walk through the jungle, calling out for the soldier until he was found.

"When they met, the office would thank the soldier, with tears in his eyes, for his loyalty and courage in continuing to defend his country for so many years.

"Then he would ask him about his experiences, and welcome him back.

"Only after some time would the soldier gently be told that the war was over, and that his country was at peace again, so that he would not have to fight any more.

"When he reached home he would be given a hero's welcome, with parades and medals, and crowds thanking him and celebrating his arduous struggle and his return and reunion with his people."

I told this story once to a class of people learning EFT, and noticed that one woman had tears spilling from her eyes as I finished. I asked her if she would be willing to talk about what she was experiencing. She said something like:

I was feeling so sorry for those soldiers, and so moved by how they were treated, and then I realized that this is how I need to treat myself. For so long I have ridiculed or criticized or tried to shut away those parts of me that react so automatically in stuck ways that I don't like myself for.

I could see how those parts of me are just like those soldiers. When I was little, the temper tantrum, or the crying might have worked, sort of, but those ways of dealing with hard times or difficult people don't work anymore. They just make things worse now! And then I just shut down, and grinned and bore it (but I wasn't doing much grinning). That doesn't work either.

I have been still fighting battles that have long since ended, and then fighting with myself for doing that. But I can't seem to stop! I get so mad at myself! But hearing this story made me realize that there are parts of me that have just been trying to protect me and keep me safe, and they have been doing their best but they just have those old tattered uniforms and rusty weapons that don't work any more.

Some part of me is probably thinking, I have been this way for so long, I think of it as just who I am. And then the scary question comes—who would I be without these behaviors? How do I know who I really am?

At least now I know that I should, and can, honor those old soldiers in me. They were just doing the best they could. And then maybe the next step will become clear.

Buried Benefits and the Highly Sensitive Person

by Joan Hitlin, MFA, CCHT

When I was 12 I had my first migraine headache. It happened while I was trying to study, but I was actually just worrying—I had two tests the next day, I'd left studying for the last minute, and there wasn't enough time to prepare for both exams.

When the migraine came, I didn't know what it was—I thought I was going blind. The next morning, instead of going to school, my mother rushed me to the eye doctor. He said I needed glasses. Meanwhile, I missed both tests.

THE 8 MASTER KEYS TO HEALING WHAT HURTS

About 3 or 4 years later, I started getting migraine headaches again, fairly regularly. I had my glasses checked, but they were OK. After a while, I noticed that I always got those migraines the night before my physics exam and never any other time! I couldn't study because I couldn't see. And then I did poorly on the exam. (Doing poorly was no surprise. I knew I was lousy in physics.)

But, here is the interesting part: I was only 15 years old. I had never heard of therapy, or of the unconscious mind. Still, somehow a light went on, and I figured out that if I got a headache I couldn't study, and if I didn't study, I had an excuse for doing poorly. *I realized that my migraine headaches were about saving face!*

So, I designed an experiment: I told myself not to have a migraine before the next test and to study hard the night before the exam, and to see what happened.

And this is what happened:
I didn't get a headache.
I studied.
I got the highest mark in the class.
(The teacher accused me of cheating, but since I was the only one with the right answers, he was the one who lost face this time!!!)

The headaches didn't come back.

This was my first-hand experience of what therapists call *Secondary Gain* (a positive by-product of an otherwise negative situation) and what I now call *Buried Benefits*. (I don't use the term Secondary Gain, because often, the benefit is the *primary* reason for the unwanted pain or habit, and not secondary at all!)

The word benefit comes from the Latin *benefacere*, meaning to do a service. *A buried benefit is performing a secret service*—giving you a hidden, eclipsed or undetected advantage that accrues from holding onto an otherwise undesirable condition.

THE 8 MASTER KEYS TO HEALING WHAT HURTS

You have a Buried Benefit if you are unknowingly holding onto:

❋ Symptoms of illness because it generates love or sympathy

❋ Physical pain because it will help win a lawsuit, or because
   it enables you to collect disability payments

❋ Excess weight because it makes you feel safe or invisible

❋ Anger because it masks grief or vulnerability

❋ Anything that keeps you from having to face situations that
   a sensitive person would rather avoid

As a highly sensitive person myself, I have often developed symptoms
that sent me rushing to my bed, or my recliner, just before I would
have had to expose myself to "sensitive situations," situations where
there was likely to be too much chaos or commotion, loud noise,
bright lights, or too many strangers.

The headaches or stomach-aches that seemed to manifest out
of nowhere were my secret schemers, helping me to get out of
overwhelming (for me) situations. The trick, of course, was learning
to consciously avoid situations that I'm just too sensitive to enjoy.
I needed to learn to turn down invitations to rock concerts and
political conventions, and to walk away from loud arguments and
smelly restaurants. I had to invoke my inner Nancy Reagan (!) and
learn to "Just Say No."

At age 15, I had unwittingly found a way to avoid the humiliation
of bad grades by generating a good excuse—"Sorry, migraine
headaches, too sick to study." When I realized what my inner
mind was up to, I was able to avoid the humiliation of bad grades
by making sure that I studied enough to do well. It was almost
comically simple.

Sometimes exposing the concealed benefit will allow the conscious,
rational mind to look at what is going on, ask "OK, what exactly is
the payoff here?" and "Is it worth the pain and suffering?"

THE 8 MASTER KEYS TO HEALING WHAT HURTS

When the payoff is identified, and then replaced by a more congruent choice, the pain or problem is often spontaneously released.

Sometimes, though, even when Buried Benefits are made conscious, it is still very hard to let go of them. Sometimes the need for the benefit is very strong, and the payoff of keeping the problem outweighs what others might assume were better alternatives.

You see, no one wants pain, but pain can bring with it certain goodies: attention, caring, demonstration of love, monetary compensation, excuses, distractions.

Buried Benefits may also be the reason why you're not moving forward in your life, even when you are really trying hard to find love, prosperity, health, fitness and happiness. You may be holding onto your stuck-ness for many reasons, most of which have to do with fear:

❊ fear of responsibility

❊ fear of new situations

❊ fear of being seen

❊ fear of failure

❊ fear of success

❊ fear of being overwhelmed

❊ fear of being found out

❊ fear of losing love

❊ fear of being over-stimulated

❊ fear of giving up guaranteed income

```
   / i°   i'°  i iv  ° v°^ >   }°^ v  ° ^°
    > °  ° ii«^°  °v  ° >   }° °
         V  v   °  °v i>
```

(I have met more than one woman, for instance, who was afraid to get a job because it would mean letting go of spousal support.)

THE 8 MASTER KEYS TO HEALING WHAT HURTS

If you have been "trying everything" to get past pain, past chronic symptoms, past addictions and cravings, and past stuck-place-syndrome, then there is a good chance that Buried Benefits are part of the problem.

Energy therapies and hypnotherapy can be of enormous help here. These are powerful modalities that go directly to the hiding places and storage spaces where Buried Benefits lurk—in the unconscious mind, and in the energy system. By dealing with Buried Benefits at the root level, by shining the bright light of day onto the previously sequestered aspects of your problems, symptoms, unwanted behaviors, and stuck places - you can create lasting change and forward movement. And you can better manage your sensitive nature.

© Joan Hitlin, 2004. Used with permission
JoanHitlin.com or Mojotivity.com

❉ ❉ ❉

What Joan in her article above is calling "Buried Benefits" is generally known in Energy Psychology as ***Psychological Reversals.**" Someone who has studied and written widely on this topic is EFT Master Lindsay Kenny. You can read more in her articles on emofree.com, NAFEH.org or EFT4ALL.com.

Both terms mean that inside all of us are some old soldiers, valiantly doing what they have been trained to do, doing their best to keep us safe and feeling strong and as worthy as possible. I truly believe that inside every limiting behavior and belief and raw emotion—all those things we blame ourselves and others for (all those shoulds!)—is a positive intention straining to get free.

Thinking this way is profound. It is life changing. I believe it is grace in action.

I have made a kind of challenge for myself to see if I can find the positive intention wherever I look. The most challenging issues that

Profoundly light-hearted strategies for unsticking stuck stuff

pop up right away of course have to do with what we call "man's inhumanity to man." Wars. Torture. Abuse. Even the phrase is interesting: the implication is that the word "humanity" actually means something good, itself. So "in-humanity" means something negative.

When I look to find the positive intention in war, for example, (without going into a politico-spiritual treatise here [it's tempting, but...next book, maybe]) I find myself thinking about the evolution of the consciousness of humanity—or perhaps the consciousness of evolution. The story of human history is, at its center, a search for love and belonging, and a sense of personal and collective sovereignty.

In more local terms, one of my favorite examples of finding the positive intention buried in bad behavior, I look to the story of Jeffery Dahmer who lived in Milwaukee in my own state of Wisconsin.

Briefly, because it is truly a grisly story (and you may not even want to read it) Jeffery grew up a terribly abused, lonely, distorted child. As an adult gay man, he sought out lovers who he eventually killed, dismembered, refrigerated and ate. He was finally caught and jailed for murder. While in jail he was killed by a fellow inmate in a fight.

How could one possibly find anything redeeming in such a person?

When I try to sense inside Jeffery Dahmer, what I find deep inside there is a desperateness, a feeling that is beyond desperate even, a bizarrely distorted seeking for love and connection. His story is an apt but terrible metaphor about connection. Truly, in his own frightening, grotesque and shattered way, Dahmer just wanted to be loved, like any of us does.

For me, his story is the ultimate test of finding positive intention hidden deep inside someone's behavior. If I can find the positive intention buried in Jeffrey Dahmer, I can find it in anyone. I often wonder what healing would have been possible for him, if—so many ifs: *if* he had been raised by less damaged parents, *if* someone

© Rue Hass 2006 ✳ 173 ✳ IntuitiveMentoring.com
Profoundly light-hearted strategies for unsticking stuck stuff

could have seen something good in him as a child, *if* someone had known EFT...

Fortunately most of us have less menacing inner soldiers than Jeffery Dahmer did, though they still manage to create plenty of difficulty for us.

Ultimately, many people who suffer from a chronic condition have this deeply unconscious but powerfully positive intention:

"In order to know that I am worthy of healing, of living, of breathing and taking up space in the world,
in order to take care of myself,
in order to be good to myself,
in order to take care of myself (stand up for myself, grow, feel safe)
I have to have this condition."

Consider your "condition." Imagine it as a kind of Dark Angel. If it were trying to get something positive for you, what would that be? Invite yourself to consider that your inner battle has been resolved.

What, if anything, comes up as a downside?
What might be uncomfortable?
What would you lose?

This will give you an indication of what these inner soldiers have been trying to fight for, all these years, on your behalf.

I asked these questions of some of the people you have already heard from in this book. Here are their answers:

NORMAN

People would expect you to do all the things that normal people do. Work a lot, take on a lot of responsibility, act like a grownup. In every moment you are making decisions about what to do and how to be, all the time. I would be faced with a whole new set of decisions. At least for awhile that would be a challenge, it would be difficult.

It is hard to break habits of identity. In your mind, who you think you are is a deep habit. Changing that I perceive as a slow process. It is not an overnight healing. Things would have to be a process. If I were to get well I would ideally arrive into it at such a rate that when I got there I would barely notice because it would have been a step-by-step process.

I wanted to get well *now* for a long time when I was younger, but now I realize it is not going to happen quickly. People who are ill with something like my disease are constantly searching for the new diet supplement, the new doctor, the new technique (including EFT), Nancy Selfridge's program (get well in five weeks!), the magic bullet that they will take and wake up and be better. It may happen for some people. For me, since this has been going on for such a long time, maybe some shifts could take place, but not an over-night idealized version of "well."

I hope for a long process of getting well, getting both better and older and more limited, all happening at the same time.

Being well is an unknown at this point. In me there's a line from a song—way back—"oh what a beautiful world, what shall I do, what shall I do," sung in great yearning and beauty.

I don't know what to do with the energy, joy and strength that I do have.

It seems all tangled up in cosmic loneliness, facing the reality of our existence in the world.

I don't think I am making this up—there is something extraordinary about being alive in the world, and what do you do with it? How do you deal with the fact that no matter how connected you feel there is a way that we are all alone? In the way other people blunt themselves with addiction, illness is easy for me to not face the challenge of being fully alive. Although it is clearly not that easy of a thing, because not everybody is that way.

The downside question—that one moment in the class when I said out loud for the first time, that for me to change I would have to change my whole identity—at that moment it seemed like it was *WHOA!*. This is not an easy thing to do! But it is good to know. It is good to know where to stand. New knowledge is always good, and understanding more is always good. EFT can take a person inward in a way that they can see and feel and understand things that they didn't before.

Not everyone felt the way Norman did:

MADELYN

It is hard to see any downsides to getting well. Looking around, I see other people doing things I can't do. Having a good time. It feels like to me that I have the worst of both worlds. For those people, because they were sick they got support. They were more open about what was happening for them. And then they didn't have to work.

But with my situation, I am not telling people about it so I am not getting any sympathy or support. I am working just hard as ever. If I was not able to continue to work, I would really have to cut back on my life style.

It is depressing—I am not getting ANY benefits. Either I have to quit working and then scale back my life, or keep working and allow myself the luxuries and benefits that come from it, but stay sick. I have the worst of both worlds. I am not getting any of the attention of compassion or extra support from being sick. It is hard to measure the downside of getting well.

I think it is sometimes very difficult to "give up the battle."

Getting "too free"?

I had been working with Inga for several weeks with her claustrophobia issue. It had lots of different aspects and memories and emotional associations, and Inga was very good at framing each of them as tappable events and themes.

In her youth she had been sexually indiscriminate, and she yearned back toward those days as representing absolute fun and freedom. However, she obsessed about having to keep herself under tight control for fear she would let loose and get too free again in irresponsible ways, and worried that she would then "be locked away forever."

She is married with two grown daughters and an active church life, all of which she felt she needed to use to keep her in the straight and narrow. Her theme was always *"I can't be who I really am. It is dangerous to express myself."*

Inga often mentioned how neglectful, critical and apparently uninterested her parents had been in her—especially her father. She felt she had to be invisible at home. The way to get her dad's approval was to be invisible, because if Inga disappeared into the woodwork, her mother didn't get her hair-trigger temper set off by her needs, and then *his* life was easier.

So we did some work with her family issues, and a lot of work on her claustrophobia, and she improved in many ways. The claustrophobia, though milder, was still there. I was beginning to wonder if we would be able to shift it. I am sure she was wondering that, too.

Profoundly light-hearted strategies for unsticking stuck stuff

Suddenly a new "doorway in" to the issue presented itself, and thankfully, I noticed it opening. Inga and I were able to put 2 and 2 and 2 together in a way that was enlightening for her:

We were working on her recent panic in the dentist's chair. She had not experienced this before, but she recognized the familiar symptoms of her claustrophobia in yet another new manifestation. As we worked, I kept hearing her talking about her dentist, how attractive he was.

On the surface this seemed like an existing detail but not a factor, but there was something about it that tugged at me, and I casually brought it into the tapping we were doing. She responded instantly, talking about how attracted she was to him, and how uncontrollably attracted she always was to men. Our work took off in this new direction.

The results were remarkable. By the end of the session she said:

"I realize now that I have been manipulating men for drama and excitement. It is like trying to get my father's attention. I have to be perfect with them. I can't be vulnerable.

"I can't let anyone know what I am really like. But I don't want to work with this!! It is the reason for my claustrophobia!!"

There were a lot of complex interconnections in those statements. We had dealt with her dentist-chair panic, but now she was suddenly facing the actual core of her obsessive claustrophobia, which had been a cover for what she described as "my obsession with men," and that was extremely threatening to her.

You can probably see that the underlying positive intention of her claustrophobia was to keep her from focusing on the much more scary area of her relationship with men—and behind that, all of the emotions and beliefs that were the result of her abusive childhood.

Inga and I had two more sessions. In the first one she came in full of sadness. She said, and this is what we worked with, "I have been mourning that I can't sleep with other men. This is my fantasy life. My fantasy life is my addiction, my obsession, my escape. The obsession with men is what I think about ALL the time; it is the core of who I am. It is the need to be acknowledged by a man (I don't want him any more after that).

"Sha says, I realize now that this obsession is who I am, but I can't tell anyone. I have to keep it hidden. My claustrophobia has been the way I keep myself under control. I keep myself from expressing who I really am, and I keep myself from actually acting on my attraction to men with my claustrophobia."

Inga came in very nervous for our next session, which turned out to be our last, for now. She knew she was facing something life-changing. I used a combination of EFT and the Core Transformation process from NLP to access and integrate the positive intention of "this core of what runs me." We ranged widely and deeply over all her issues, among them:

* her obsession with men and sexuality and how she experienced it in her body
* its intention to protect her and make her feel safe when she never felt safe
* her feeling of unworthiness
* her need to feel accepted
* her desire to feel like it was OK to be successful
* it was OK to feel successful
* wanting to get noticed for her successes
* her intention to deal with her issues around her mother who "needed us to need her"

Profoundly light-hearted strategies for unsticking stuck stuff

THE 8 MASTER KEYS TO HEALING WHAT HURTS

❋ the importance of making her dad happy by being
   invisible to him
❋ her belief that "the world doesn't like it when you
   express yourself"
❋ wanting to have the freedom to be expressive
❋ and more…

At the end of the session she said (I tried to write it down word for word because it was so articulate):

I feel a center in myself now, and I can imagine the feeling of happiness emerging from this center."

I feel easy. My brain is no longer in overdrive. This is such an easy, comfortable way to live your life. Now when I am around men, if I move and act and speak freely I might find from them more of the sense of connection that I have actually been looking for. I can imagine men being drawn to me, seeking me out in a different way from how it has been. I could just be comfortable around them.

I can imagine a way of being around men that invites them to be more of who they are too, and it doesn't have to lead to sex. This can be even better than sex!

I need now to focus less on men. They won't be on my radar like they have been. But I don't have to exclude men from my life. When I do express myself (Inga is an artist and a musician) and get criticisms, I can understand that it is about that person, and not about me. I can look at it not personally.

When I came in today I was so worried about what would I do
   ° my obsession.

      Who would I be? How would I know how to act?"

But at the same time I have been eager to change. Now I see how a lot of the elements of my life were tied up together. It is like making

Profoundly light-hearted strategies for unsticking stuck stuff

a cake. I wove in some comments about baking a new cake, and having your cake and eating it too! Inga laughed.

This is more of the email exchange between Sally and me that took place over about a two-month period. Sally had been learning about what she called her "pain producer," and how it did its job: keeping her from focusing on and feeling her childhood emotional abuse. In between emails we had fairly frequent telephone sessions, in each session tapping for the issues in Sally's past that were troubling her and leading to her current chronic pain. (See reports of earlier sessions in Chapter 3)

SALLY

I am very glad we went ahead and had the last session we had, even though my husband's dad was dying. The grief didn't start until the day after we talked. On Friday they "pulled the plugs" out of the life support that was keeping his dad alive. He never regained consciousness and died within a half hour.

Why I am glad is that I was able to get the negative things "out of the way," leaving me more able to appreciate the good things about my father-in-law, and there were some good things, most notably my husband. I don't feel the anger anymore, and in a strange way I am seeing parallels between his dad and my dad.

The major difference between them being that his dad could love unconditionally and show it, and my dad had a real problem with that. My husband's father was a very affectionate man. I never really liked him, but I did love him. Thank you, Sally

THE 8 MASTER KEYS TO HEALING WHAT HURTS

Last Thursday my family doctor called to tell me that my bone scan "confirmed" the x-ray findings - that there was some loosening of the hip prosthesis I received during partial hip replacement surgery in April 2004. This immediately got me thinking more about my hip than about my chronic pain. I did some research on the internet and found out that putting in a new hip replacement (called revision surgery) would be a much more complicated, lengthy and dangerous operation and would likely not yield as good an outcome as the first surgery.

Among the causes listed for loosening was infection. I blanched at this because I had been very lax about using preventive antibiotics before dental work, gyn exams, etc. I convinced myself this was all my fault and I'd have to pay for it by having revision surgery.

At this point I think my pain producer was getting quite interested. Here was a perfectly dreadful physical ailment I was sure I had. All my attention was fixed on it. Why bother, (my pain producer said), with giving me lots of the old chronic pain. Possible surgery was a lot more novel and intimidating than plain old pain.

So the pain producer decided to take a little time off and give me less pain. Even after I saw the orthopedic surgeon, who disagreed with the test results, I was still being examined for other causes of the thigh pain. I would need to have an MRI and wait a month to see what developed. So, the pain producer can have a little vacation until this blows over.

Something similar happened to me when I broke my hip. During the hospital stay and my recuperation I had very little chronic pain. I think it was for the same reason. The pain producer didn't need to try to hog my attention. The hip problem was taking all my time and attention. I also think that it is quite possible that our work together is helping to heal the problems that the pain producer has been trying to keep me from thinking about. And I am sure that continuing work will help even more. Love, Sally

Profoundly light-hearted strategies for unsticking stuck stuff

Just as soon as I got off the phone with you, John asked me what you thought of my vision, and I realized that I had forgotten to tell you.

Again, it was just as I was starting to fall asleep. I saw myself in a room. I was walking toward one of the walls and I walked right through it. It seemed to dissolve to let me through. John's immediate interpretation was that it showed me able to overcome a seemingly overwhelming obstacle to find health, healing, happiness, all good things. That seems like a very good interpretation to me. Love, Sally

GOLD IN THE TOWERS:
Finding the Positive Intention in Trauma

The attack on the World Trade Center and the Pentagon affected all of us. Nothing will be the same. How can we integrate such profound and frightening change?

A bit of guidance for me came a few days after the event, when a friend showed me the Tower card from a Tarot deck. This traditional version showed a tall gray tower, surrounded by black clouds and lightning, its top crashing over in flames. Two figures are falling through the air, upside down, limbs akimbo. It looked exactly like the images I had been seeing continually on television.

This card signals a breakdown of all the long-established patterns and assumptions that we have taken for granted. It says that a cataclysmic force is making us let go of the limited vision of reality that blocks our understanding and our perception of truth.

One Tarot deck describes the Tower like this: "A beautiful city rises in elaborately constructed towers, representing plans and projects, things that are established, ordered and controlled. A violent storm sweeps over the city, striking the tall towers with sudden bolts of lightning…. Old structures are changing, like it or not…. You are being blasted from one reality to the next, and the way is being cleared for transformation. Change is in the air, crackling in the atmosphere like summer lightning."

Many of the people I worked with following the attacks experienced just such an opening to deep change.

One woman was extremely disturbed by the images of people jumping from the WTC buildings. She found herself obsessively glued to the news all that long day. However, she is a mother of two little boys, and they were constantly pulling at her attention. She was horrified to find herself wishing, for the first time, that they had never been born, desperately wanting crawl into a hole and die, away from the terror and panic and destruction.

This woman had grown up with a highly functioning, but severely mentally ill, mother who was a Holocaust survivor. "My mother ran in panic from real and then-imagined bombs, all her life. Being alive was hell for her," she said. Her mother jumped from a high-rise building to her death five years ago, having, for all of my client's life, threatened suicide, begged to die.

My client realized that her role in her mother's life had been to keep her alive, emotionally pulling her back from jumping out of her life—in the same way, she suddenly understood, that her sons were now doing for her.

It was a huge revelation for her. "I thought she was rejecting me, all my life. I thought there was something wrong with me, all my life. I have understood in an hour today what my mother never was able to experience in 20 years of therapy with the best psychiatrists in the country. But this never would have happened if there hadn't been an event of this magnitude to push me into it. All this death. But I can be alive now."

My friend who showed me the Tower card pointed out the pieces of gold that were falling as the tower came down. She said, "Whenever this card comes up in a reading, I always tell people that, in order for the inner gold to fall to earth and seed itself, you have to 'blow your mind.' Your life-limiting beliefs are getting blown apart. Otherwise, the gold is caught inside, and can't be used."

The World Trade Center was all about gold.

David Spangler is a modern day mystic, philosopher, teacher, wise-man, also a father and a very grounded loving funny man who lives with his wife and four children in the Seattle area. Soon after the attacks he offered, from his inner awareness, a message that out-frames these events in a beautiful, graceful way.

He begins: "What has taken place is an act of sacrifice and a gift given by the Soul of America to the world at large."
(Now, these words will resonate with each of us in different ways. The deep meaning of sacrifice is "to make sacred, holy".

Soul of America … into me comes an image of a great and powerful presence of light hovering over, under and through our nation, like wings, a presence that is made up of the best of each of us, that reaches beyond us to the source of life itself. There is a deep silence, and a feeling of belonging, a feeling of warmth and comfort and safety that is different from the safety of my body.)

David's message says that whenever a death occurs, there is an energy of spirit that is released into life. This energy is neutral, and its use may be shaped. If love is present in the last moments of life, even if the death is violent or the result of hateful acts, the powerful gift of energy remains. We have heard so many stories of the love and courage expressed and demonstrated by people in each of those tragic and terrible situations. The importance of this gift cannot be underestimated.

He talks about the "reservoir" of hate and fear, the pain and suffering and anger in our world, that all peoples contribute to and are responsible for, in so many little and large acts on a daily basis everywhere. This is a human problem, not a tribal or national one, and as humans we are held accountable for our acts of violence.

It is as if these negative energies are circling the earth, seeking a place to land, to discharge, like lightning.   From his perspective, he saw that the Soul of America took on the inner work of receiving the blow of this energy, because it was strong enough to transmute it.
In fact, he felt that this act has prevented, for the time being, much worse acts. All of those deaths, held in a love and courage that went beyond the fear and pain, have released a deep blessing, an inner gold, a source of blessing for ourselves and others.

David's view is that many of the people who died had, in an inner way, chosen to be a part of this sacrifice. For those who didn't specifically choose this death, still it was a part of their destiny in ways and for reasons that were personal to them. And he was clear that "all who died were immediately embraced by the love that led the Soul of America to offer itself in this way, and their entry…was graced and blessed by this spirit."

His message concludes: "… in the opening of the portal so powerfully by the deaths of so many, this gift of life from death, even though initiated by the hatred of a few, became a channel for an outpouring of the love that is at the heart of America. It is, I know, a painful gift, but it is a gift nonetheless."

It is for us who remain to take that gift and reshape our world with it.

It is a precious thing, and it can remake our world. It is a grace for us to embody.

10
THE TRUTH ABOUT YOU

The TRUTH about Me

I UNDERSTAND the TRUTH about me
I AM of value! I AM worthy!
I deserve to trust, love & believe in myself

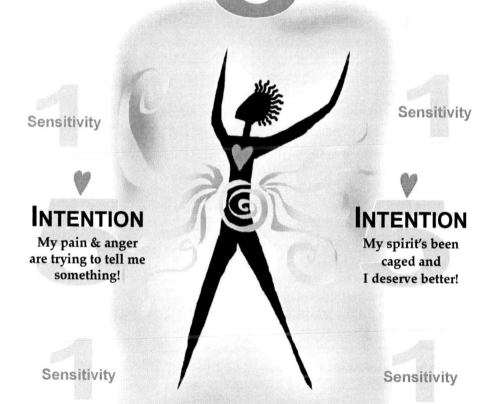

Sensitivity

Sensitivity

INTENTION
My pain & anger
are trying to tell me
something!

INTENTION
My spirit's been
caged and
I deserve better!

Sensitivity

Sensitivity

6 - The Truth about you:

Out of the positive intention, and its meaning for you, create a new belief that feels good to you.

> "Carefully watch your thoughts,
> for they become your words.
>
> Manage and watch your words,
> for they will become your actions.
>
> Consider and judge your actions,
> for they have become your habits.
>
> Acknowledge and watch your habits,
> for they shall become your values.
>
> Understand and embrace your values,
> for they become your destiny."

Mahatma Gandhi

In these chapters we have learned how our bodies are an instant feedback system.

We have learned how to read our emotions and our physical symptoms. That they signal our awareness, letting us know how close we are—or how far off course—to manifesting a life that reflects our best possibilities and capacities and destiny.

I believe that we do know what is truly right for us, but that we may be asleep to that. We may be caught in a different dream. The dream

Profoundly light-hearted strategies for unsticking stuck stuff

we are caught in might have us playing out stories with a more "hopeless, helpless, worthless" theme. So our job here is to learn how to awaken to a deeper truth.

Within each of us is a knowing of the Truth of who we *are* that both transcends and goes deeper than the often painful story we tell ourselves about who we are in the world and what it means for us to be here. This Truth is our image of our spiritual presence, our essential Self.

In our hands, EFT can be a spiritual tool that assists people in awakening to the power and gift of their own sacred sovereignty as a human being.

I believe that my job as a practitioner is fundamentally to tune in to a client's soul, to the brightest and best in them, to their deepest positive intention, and hold the space for that person, mirroring it for them, until they can access and enter it on their own, at will.

This is energy work in the deepest sense. EFT is a wonderful tool for helping a person to clear away any obstructions to moving into this space and just inhabiting it as a right. You might even say (I would!) it is our divine right to know this Truth.

The bravest, most open minded and open-hearted of our scientists have been coming to the same conclusions about what we humans are, who we are in relation to each other and to the earth itself, and what is possible for life in the universe.

David Bohm
The latest research in physics by people like University of London physicist David Bohm, is suggesting that objective reality does not exist, that even though it seems solid to us, the universe is essentially a gigantic and magnificently detailed hologram.

The "whole in every part" nature of a hologram provides us with a new way of understanding organization and order. Western science has always thought that the best way to understand something, whether a frog or an atom, is to dissect it and study its respective parts.

But a hologram teaches us that if we try to take apart something that is constructed holographically, we will not get the pieces of it, we will only get smaller wholes. Now we know that every part of a hologram contains all the information possessed by the whole.

Bohm believes that at some deep level of reality the subatomic particles of the universe are not individual entities, but are actually extensions of the same "fundamental something."

He offers this wonderfully evocative illustration:

He invites us to imagine an aquarium containing a fish. But we can't actually see the aquarium directly—everything we know about it comes from two television cameras, one directed at the front of the aquarium and the other directed at its side. It looks to us like the fish on each of the screens are separate entities.

As we watch the two fish, we can begin to see that there is a relationship between them. Whatever the one does, the other does as well, but with slight differences. For instance, one may always face to the front and the other is always seen from the side. It even might look like the two fish are communicating with each other. But there is only one fish.

Using this analogy, Bohm explains that the apparent faster-than-light connection between subatomic particles is really telling us that there is a deeper level of reality that we are not consciously aware of. We see things as separate because we are seeing only a portion of their reality. Bohm believes that the universe is itself a projection, an indivisible hologram.

❊　❊　❊

Profoundly light-hearted strategies for unsticking stuck stuff

Karl Pribram

Stanford neurophysiologist Karl Pribram has a similar theory for the brain. Pribram believes memories are encoded in patterns of nerve impulses, like patterns of laser light on a piece of film containing a holographic image. In other words, Pribram believes the brain is itself a hologram.

A hologram functions as a sort of lens that is able to convert an apparently meaningless blur of frequencies into a coherent image.

Pribram believes the brain is also like a lens that translates the frequencies it receives through the senses into the inner world of our perceptions.

It is mind-boggling to put Pribram's holographic model of the brain together with Bohm's theory. If the world isn't as concrete as we thought, and if what is "out there" is actually a holographic blur of frequencies, and if the brain is also a hologram and only selects some of the frequencies out of this blur and transforms them into sensory perceptions, what becomes of objective reality?

It ceases to exist! So the bottom line is that we are really "receivers" floating through a "kaleidoscopic sea of frequency."

Amit Goswami

Consciousness at this earth level seems to have the capacity to become a physical reality that is only one channel on the multi-dial of the super-hologram of the cosmos. In other words, as physicist Amit Goswami says in the film *"What the Bleep Do We Know:"*

```
"/ i i° ^° °...    ° i i‰ °  ° i it»
 i   }° ^°V  ^V  ^ i^^]°‵^  i‵°°
7 i°> i°>  °>  i]°>  ‵° i°> i°>  ° i°
```

He came to this conclusion over a period of many years. Goswami tells the wonderful story of how he was working for years just doing the routine approach to having a career as a scientist: doing research, publishing papers, getting grants—science as a "professional trip."

Finding himself feeling desperately stuck and stopped in his life, he realized that he had lost the really satisfying way of experiencing science, which is the spirit of discovery, the curiosity, the spirit of knowing truth.

In his search for truth and the nature of reality, Goswami took up meditation. He also, along the way, fell in love. He found himself opening to ideas that he says take Bohm's thinking to the next level, and a "new way of doing science."

In realist theory, he says, everything can be explained through mathematical equations. In other words, in reality theory there is no freedom of choice. Even spiritually-oriented science was asking questions like, "How can you do science if you let consciousness do things which are 'arbitrary'?" He struggled with that because he was convinced that there is real freedom of choice.

In a sudden moment of awareness he came to the conclusion that "consciousness is the ground of all being."

Goswami describes staying up that night after this moment of realization, looking at the sky, in the afterglow of his inner opening. It came to him that seeing consciousness as the ground of all being would inspire new thinking in both science and spirituality—and that had been his aim since he had been a child. He grew up in India, the son of a spiritual leader, reading Einstein, wanting to find a scientific way to describe what he learned from his father.

This moment took place in the late 1980's, and Goswami says that since then he has been "just blessed with ideas after ideas, and lots of problems have been solved—the problem of cognition, perception, biological evolution, mind-body healing."

His first book about these ideas was *The Self Aware Universe: How Consciousness Creates the Material World,* and his latest is called *Physics of the Soul*. Imagine how much fun he must have had writing a book with Deepak Chopra called *The Visionary Window: the Quantum Physicist's Guide to Enlightenment*.

To me, all of this means that when we do EFT, or any energetic healing work (and at some level all healing is energy work) and someone lights up inside from an insight, we are changing the entire universe.

Right before I wrote those last words, a client called and said that for the first time in her life she is beginning to feel a sensation of lightness inside. This is scary to her—as a product of an extremely abusive childhood, she was now experiencing herself and the world differently than she always had. She wanted to know if this was OK (!), and was it also OK to still have inner fears at the same time?

I assured her that feeling lightness inside was a good thing, and that it is natural to have all those possible emotions available at the same time. And that our job, once we realize that we have options, is to pick the station that *we choose* to listen to. She hung up, reassured.

The universe just got a little bit better for all of us!

Butterflies and Imaginal Disks

Another of our open-hearted, lyrical scientists is Dr. Elisabet Sahtouris. She is an Evolution Biologist, Futurist and Commissioner for the *World Commission on Global Consciousness and Spirituality* (GlobalSpirit.org).

Every time I read or listen to her speak, she manages to transform science for me into a magical image of Truth in action, radiant with the story of life evolving and how important each of us is to the journey.

She offers these evocative thoughts: ❈

The really exciting thing about being alive today is that we're all here for a great transformation. It's clear that we're unsustainable. We have to change things and we're figuring out how.

And in a sense the old system is getting more entrenched, more violent, more powerful. It's trying to keep itself alive, while we know that we need a new system.

The best metaphor I've found about this situation comes from the biological world again. It's the metamorphosis of a caterpillar into a butterfly. You could see the old system as a caterpillar crunching its way through the eco-system, eating up to three hundred times its weight in a single day, bloating itself until it just can't function anymore, and then going to sleep with its skin hardening into a chrysalis.

What happens in its body is that little imaginal disks (as they're called by biologists) begin to appear in the body of the caterpillar, and its immune system attacks them. But they keep coming up stronger and they start to link with each other.

As they connect, as they link with each other, they mature into fully-fledged cells, and more and more of them aggregate until the immune system of the caterpillar just can't function any more. At that point the body of the caterpillar melts into a nutritive soup that can feed the butterfly.

I love this metaphor, which I first heard from Norie Huddle, author of the children's book *Butterfly*, because it shows us why, first of all, we who want to change the world are co-existing with the old system for a while, and why there's no point in attacking the old system, because you know the caterpillar is unsustainable so it's going to die. What we have to focus on is "can we build a viable butterfly?"

We can put our energy into building all the alternative ways of doing things that we know we want for a loving world. The kind of world we talk about in this Commission. How do we wake people up to understand that we're spiritual beings having human experiences? We can learn from nature how to go about this process of evolution that's called for today. We can build alternatives to the old models of education, of law, of healthcare. All of this we're doing.

We know we can function as a global family because we've got communication systems that are global. Even if wars are going on we see that we can send faxes and make phone calls and be on the Internet. The Internet, by the way, functions like a real self-organizing living system. You have to tolerate a lot of chaos in that situation to see the good things emerging, to see us connecting more and more, and that's happening.

So I have tremendous hope for all of us humans together, using our creative technology, our computers, in order to link each other—linking our minds, our concepts, our visions. Above all we need a very powerful vision to hold that butterfly image for us. To know where we want to go. Because the old system is very clear about what it wants. And we really do create our realities out of our beliefs.

If we don't believe in a positive world in which all humans are liberated to express their creativity, we cannot build it.

We must hold the vision very clearly and then go about doing whatever each of us loves doing most, knowing that the others will do the other parts.

None of us has to do the whole thing. Together we can really make it happen.

Ratical.org/LifeWeb/Articles/AfterDarwin.html#fn11
and Sahtouris.com
Reprinted with permission

❋ ❋ ❋

Choosing a station to listen to: changing channels

Recently I had a first telephone session with a 79 year-old woman who has had a long history of severe chronic conditions, including arthritis and Parkinson's Disease. Her voice was low and saturated with sadness. She has seen many practitioners of all kinds over the years, as have most people with long standing pain who go from doctor to doctor, healer to healer. Eve had been referred to me by a massage therapist who had heard of EFT and thought it might be an option for her. In the course of our initial conversation, I heard her say, "I don't feel I have a future."

Instead of going right to EFT I thought we would begin with this belief. It contained such a profound sense of hopelessness and worthlessness. I was thinking that our efforts to make a difference in what hurts for her would not get very far if our work was taking place within this frame. She needed to know the truth about herself!

I began by asking Eve to imagine that there was a path that started right from her feet, and she could make it look and feel however she wanted to. Her path was sand, she said right away, and it followed the edge of the sea. I asked her to imagine it stretching ahead, and she found it went on until she could no longer see it.

She was clearly good at imagining, and nothing was blocking her ability to do that, so we spent a little time creating beauty along her path, to let her know that good things were there for her. I didn't specifically say that this path led to her future; I just let the imagery speak to the part of Eve that was walking this path.

As our connection was becoming more established, and I could feel Eve warming to possibility, we began to do a process I call "Creating the Map of the History of Your Future."

I asked, *"If your childhood were a story, what would the title be?"* She said promptly, *"The Little Match Girl."* Perhaps you remember this Hans Christian Anderson story, written in 1846, which begins: "Most terribly cold it was; it snowed, and was nearly quite dark, and evening—the last evening of the year. In this cold and darkness there went along the street a poor little girl, bareheaded, and with naked feet. When she left home she had slippers on, it is true; but what was the good of that? They were very large slippers, which her mother had hitherto worn; so large were they; and the poor little thing lost them as she scuffled away across the street, because of two carriages that rolled by dreadfully fast.

"One slipper was nowhere to be found; the other had been laid hold of by an urchin, and off he ran with it; he thought it would do capitally for a cradle when he some day or other should have children himself. So the little maiden walked on with her tiny naked feet, which were quite red and blue from cold. She carried a quantity of matches in an old apron, and she held a bundle of them in her hand. Nobody had bought anything of her the whole livelong day; no one had given her a single farthing.

"She crept along trembling with cold and hunger – a very picture of sorrow, the poor little thing!"

I asked Eve what the *themes of this story* were. She said, "Hopeless. Naive. Wishful. Stupid. Gullible."

I was guessing that she was not thinking of the end of the story about the little match-seller. True, in the actual story, the little girl dies, but what if we think of this story as a metaphor? She uses her own light (her matches) to become transported by her inner guardian in the form of her grandmother, to an inner place where she can see herself in the warmth and richness and value and vitality of a greater light.

(NOTE: Please, always replace my words and concepts about spiritual matters with your own ways of describing such transformations so that it is congruent with your beliefs. Don't let yourself be put off by my way of describing things! Find your way.)

As a path toward discovering her own "Self-light," I asked Eve what had she *loved to do as a child?* She said she loved to swing slowly on the swings, daydreaming, imagining herself becoming a famous violinist, or a beautiful figure skater, or becoming rich and giving away millions. (Do we have a Sensitive Idealist-Healer here or what?)

In her actual childhood life, Eve was raised by a single mother who was emotionally disturbed and depressed, who valued only hard work, and who required that Eve take care of *her*. Eve had to leave school at 16 to support her mother. She had to give her mother all her earnings.

I asked Eve to list her current concerns. They centered around not having a future, never feeling smart enough or worth anything, and feeling that she didn't ever deserve even the little that she was getting.

Her biggest concern was that she wanted to take care of herself—she didn't want to have to go into a nursing home. Her children had offered to take her in, but she felt they were so busy with young families and problems of their own—she didn't want to burden them.

The title for her list of present concerns was "**Zero.**"

It's 3-6 months from now
and you are noticing good changes

The next question I asked Eve was to imagine that she and I had been working together for a few months, and that she was noticing changes in herself that felt good to her. What new behaviors, self-talk, different feelings in her body were letting her know, in this near-future time now, that she was changing in ways that were right for her?

This was hard for her to imagine. As I was searching for a way to engage Eve's imagination on her own behalf, something she said prompted me to ask her what she had done for her work in her life.

She said she had been a teacher. Over the years she had taught the whole gamut, from kindergarten through high school.

Following my intuition, I said something like, "Well, you know that in any classroom there is a range of students, from the ones who are positive and easy to work with, to the ones whose actions and words create major challenges for you and everyone else?" She chuckled and agreed.

And, I went on, "The best teachers are always talking about being on the lookout for the 'teachable moment,' and 'catching them being good,' when they have difficult students. When you were a teacher, what would you want those difficult kids to notice about themselves?"

"I wanted them to notice and believe that they could do anything." Eve said, passionately.

I continued, thinking aloud, "What if you imagine all those voices in *you* as a classroom full of different kinds of students, both positive and negative. If you set yourself in the direction of 'catching *yourself* being good,' what would you find yourself noticing about *you*?"

She began to talk about her love for and from her favorite granddaughter, a four-year-old named Grace. "I can feel her love all over," Eve said.

Since she was talking about feeling something positive in her body, I wanted to amplify this, so I asked her to describe where in her body she felt this, and what it felt like.

Imagine that you are someone

who is noticing *and honoring* these changes.

Then I asked Eve to imagine she could float over and down into Grace, imagine that she *was* Grace, imagine that she was feeling and thinking and seeing *as* Grace. I thanked "Grace" for being here, and

I said, "Grace, I know that since you are such a smart girl, and you love your grandma so much, you have probably noticed that your grandma has been feeling a lot better than she used to. Tell me, what do you notice about her?"

As Grace, Eve said, "Grandma can walk! She is doing more things. She is very pretty. She shines! I feel how happy she is. When my Grandma holds my hand she is magic! She is happy and light and sparkly, and she looks like God!" Eve's voice was alight with love.

I thanked Grace (thinking, **really** good job, Grace!), and invited Eve to thank her too. I told Eve to float out of Grace's little body (and big awareness!), sending Grace gently back to where she was, and for Eve to come back into her own body bringing with her all of Grace's knowing about who Eve really was.

What is the title for the story of your near future?

What was the title of this story, I asked? It was, *"I Thought I Couldn't Do It, But I Can Do Anything!"*

Completing the legacy of your life

Next I asked Grace to imagine herself as really old, not as dying but as completing the leaving of the legacy of her life on the earth. How old would she be?

"100!" was the instant reply.

So, what did she look like now at 100, where did she live, with whom? And more importantly, what was she like now? I asked her to imagine that she had now had 21 years—a long time!—to live into and deepen all those lovely images that Grace had offered of who Eve really was inside, once she began to change into the realization of it.

I loved her reply. It flowed slowly and thoughtfully from her heart right into words:

"I wear what I like. I am not influenced or required by anyone but me. These are God's rules. They are good rules. I do not have to speak to people for them to know that I love them. I have taught this to Grace. She is beautiful and creative. I don't need anyone, but I have everyone. I have gotten much better at asking for help."

When I asked her about the legacy that her life is leaving on the earth, how the earth is a better place for her life having been part of it, she said:

"My children and my grandchildren and my great-grand-children will ask themselves when they make a major decision, "Would Grandma feel good about this?" They will want to live lives that better the world. They will want and know how to do this because of me."

Title your legacy

Her title for Eve at 100 years old was *"I Am Making a Difference."*

What are you doing right now
that is leading to your legacy?

For the last step in this process, I asked Eve to come all the way back to the present moment. As she looked forward in her life toward her future, and "I Am Making a Difference," what was she doing *right now* that was leading to this future? Little things...big things...thoughts? I reminded her what I knew she knew already, that every single thought we have, and every action that we take, creates our future.

She said, "I am always looking at what I do to see if it is fitting into the idea that I am making a difference. I am thinking healing, loving, giving thoughts. I am calling you. I am rereading healing messages. I am listening to my positive thinking tapes. I am following my intuition. And I am having a lot of communication with Grace! Maybe I am even going to visit her! I am taking care of myself."

Mmmm!, better than thinking you have *no* future, I thought. Her title for this present time of initiating positive actions and thoughts to build her future with was *"Every Little Bit Helps."*

Title the whole saga of your life

Finally, the last title I asked Eve for was a title for the whole saga, that began with "The Little Match Girl," went to "Zero," and then to "Every Little Bit Helps," and then to, "I Thought I Couldn't Do It But I Can Do Anything!" and finished with "I Am Making a Difference."

The title of Eve's saga was: *"A Good Life."*

As we completed our session, I thanked Eve for the privilege of working with God!

Now, imagine that *you* had begun life as "The Little Match Girl." Now you sense that what you are beginning to transform is what you are weaving from your own thoughts and actions.

What new belief, what new truth will you choose as a loom to spin your most creative thoughts and actions upon?

(With thanks to psychologist and NLP trainer Michael Banks for the idea upon which this process was based.)

Health follows joy

A woman in a workshop recently said, "My life is so boring and empty. I don't ever do anything. And I don't feel good. But I can't do anything that would make me happy until I feel better. I have to get healthy first."

I suggested that she might seek out ways of bringing joy into her life *first*—that health follows from happiness."

"No," she said, as if she hadn't even heard me (and she hadn't!), "I have to get healthy first. I am not even sleeping well. First I have to sleep better. I can't find any joy in life until I deal with my health."

I repeated what I had said about finding joy first, with more emphasis. Others were nodding their heads. But it still didn't register. I was in this workshop as a participant, not the facilitator, so it wasn't really my place to take this belief up with her. I really thought about it a lot though.

SALLY

This email came from my client, Sally:

I had a short nervous breakdown in the shower this afternoon, when *the enormity of what I had given up in order to be taken care of* hit me very hard. It's not like I never had this thought before, but I certainly had not had it with the same emotional force before. It was overpowering grief.

What came out of it was, "Even though I am very, very sorry for what I have given up in order to be taken care of, I deeply, etc. and I intend to completely and utterly forgive myself.

In our telephone session later I asked Sally, "What specifically do you feel that you have given up in order to be taken care of?"

She said, "I have given up:

❋   any sense of independence

THE 8 MASTER KEYS TO HEALING WHAT HURTS

* my ability to travel
* my ability to have a job
* my ability to have a decent sex life

I have given up so much of my life and identity in order to be taken care of! Sometimes I despair that the pain will never go away!"
As I listened to Sally, I was hearing her speaking from an identity of helpless victim.

I knew she had spent most of the last 20 years of her life deepening into this feeling, while at the same time desperately seeking a way out of it. She has been to all the medical experts, done all the therapy, explored some alternative approaches.

I wondered—what if she changed the meaning of her pain? What if she literally changed the meaning of her identity as a helpless person with pain?

I asked her. "Sally, what if you could change how you describe yourself from Helpless Victim to something else?   What if you could 'have it all,' so to speak? What if you could have a sense of being independent, as well as a feeling that you are living a good life, and have the pain too, if necessary… or sometimes… or—whatever evolved? What would that be like?"

Sally was baffled, nonplussed, stymied, stuck. She couldn't imagine, yet, what I was talking about.

I continued: You have set up this equation for your life:
First I must get rid of my pain, *then* I can have my life back.

My Identity: I am a helpless person in pain who needs to be taken care of.

How I should proceed: Get rid of pain—Get to have a life—Get to be happy and feel good.

THE 8 MASTER KEYS TO HEALING WHAT HURTS

Or, in other words:

6 n̊o pain—then I get to   " What I want to—then I get to   °
happy."

Offering a radical alternative to this approach to life, I continued:

"What if you can find ways to Get a Life that feels good to you right
now, so you just have that, and no matter what happens, you know
how to maintain that sense of goodness in your life. Might that
change the meaning of your pain, and the experience of your pain,
and the meaning of your life? Try this other equation on for a fit:

My Identity:
I am in charge of my own life and my own choices. I care for myself.

How I could proceed:
Find ways to   ° > « « ° > ` ° v i i  ° }  ` °   " 7 p what I enjoy in my
life—then I will   6 lêss pain, (or maybe none!)

In other words:

° > « « °   ] °

" ° > ° ° >   °   ] °

6   ° i ˆ ˆ ° « >

"So, Sally. Say some more about what your identity would be in *this*
context?"

Sally was thoughtful for a moment, and then she said, "I am thinking
of times when my pain actually did disappear for awhile. There
was that time at my father's 90th birthday party. Event though
my relationship with him had always been rocky, and he now had
Alzheimer's Disease and was able to be even less present for me that he
had been earlier in his life, I had invited all the people that had been
close to our family over the years.

"There were no strangers there, I could be myself, and I was very absorbed in talking with people. I was not conscious of my pain for that whole time, even though I was sitting—and I feel pain most often in my buttocks."

She went on, thinking aloud: "Hmmm… When I become so engaged in some activity, or I am creating something that I am enjoying, or I am involved in some satisfying interpersonal situation, I think I lose my sense of pain. I concentrate on something outside myself.

"When I am with people I feel comfortable with…for example at my cousin's for Christmas—it was a 4-5 hour period, and I was sitting that whole time. I kept sitting, and my pain didn't even start. Or another time when I was with my two oldest friends—again, no pain for an extended time."

I asked her what it was that was consistent in all those situations?

"In all those situations, I could just be myself. I have spent so much of my life being what others expected me to be!

"It got to the point where my body and my mind rebelled. There were early warning signs, pains, discomforts, illness, but I ignored them. I SAT on them! I squelched them. I wasn't going to let them stop me!

"Ohhhh…! The pain I feel right now—this is how much it hurts to keep myself from being who I am."

"So," I asked, "Who are you?"

Sally was stumped again. She had no idea how to answer this question. She had, after all, spent her life being what other people wanted her to be.

Profoundly light-hearted strategies for unsticking stuck stuff

The Narnia Technique

I was thinking of the scene in the first book of the *Chronicles of Narnia*, by C.S. Lewis: The four children have been virtually orphaned by the bombing in London during WWII. Like thousands of other children who were wrenched from their families and their lives and sent to outlying places of refuge, these four have found themselves in a huge old house in the country. It is a forbidding place, with a stern housekeeper and a stern, scary (they think) old man.

Trying to find ways of coping with this frightening situation, the children at one point get up a game of hide and seek.

The youngest child, Lucy, hides in a big old wardrobe, full of coats. Pushing to the back of the wardrobe, she discovers that it opens into a different land, a different dimension even. A different place, different rules, different and unknown people, but clearly rich with resources (even though the wicked Ice Queen has the land in thrall of winter just now).

I asked Sally to imagine that she has done something similar. Imagine that she has stepped into another environment altogether, one that is guided by, say, the Queen of Summer and Abundance of all Good Things. Now, here she is in a new and wonderful environment, where she can create herself anew. No one knows her here. There are no expectations of her. And the place is full of wonderful interesting things to do.

"What would you do here?" I asked her. "What would you find yourself drawn to do in this paradise?

"Would you be drawn to people? If so, how would you know which ones to approach? What are your clues?"

Sally thought she would be looking for people who were interested in what she was interested in: the arts, the theater, genealogy. "People who have a good sense of humor," she mused, getting into this.

"People who can laugh at themselves, who don't take themselves too seriously. People who have interesting stories to tell. People who are good listeners. Someone who is interested in *me*!"

Those were good clues.

But then Sally, said, "Oh, but now that brings up my shyness! I can't just go out and meet people!"

"So how would you take care of that?" I asked her.

"Ummm, well... I could tap for feeling more comfortable facing a new person. I could make sure I was connecting with people who are like me, people who feel safe to me. I guess if I pay attention to how I feel when I am with someone, and if it feels like they are genuinely interested in me, and if I find them interesting as well—I don't think I would be so shy. It might even be fun!

"Maybe if I looked for people and activities that I actually enjoy, instead feeling I have to meet all these expectations..." her voice trailed off in thoughtfulness.

I asked Sally what she might have fun doing together with these people? She said they might go out to dinner, go to the movies, the theater, even the circus (!).

I asked her, "What lights up in you when you do these activities with people you enjoy?" Sally said she likes the intellectual challenge, the stimulation of the conversations.

"Now," I said, "when you are doing activities that you love with people that you love, how does it make you *feel* inside?"

"I feel a good feeling in my tummy. A warm, soft, satisfying feeling, like having finished a yummy, wonderful wonderful meal, where I didn't eat too much, and I feel just right."

I pointed out that this kind of feeling was probably there when she did activities that were fun and creative on her own, as well.

Sally mentioned that she had been thinking of taking a drawing class, and that she got the same kind of feeling when she thought of doing that. (We acknowledged that she had tools like EFT, and resources like me, for dissolving the feelings of meeting expectations that might come up in the class.)

We did a little guided visualization, allowing that warm good feeling to fill her body, and adding the feeling of lighting up inside when she was doing something Sally loved with people that she loved. We asked her body to remember this YUM feeling.

I suggested to Sally that she could use the YUM feeling as a signal. She could ask her body to be an inner guide, a wise ally, in the process of filling her life with good sensations. She could hold some person, or activity, or thought inside herself for consideration, and notice whether she got this YUM feeing. If she did, it was a go.

If she didn't get a YUM feeling, or maybe even got a more YUCK feeling, she could ask herself, What does this situation need in order to produce a YUM feeling?

And then she could start using her imagination (another good inner ally) to help her to add some YUM—or lots of YUM—let's be dramatically generous with ourselves!

At last, Sally could now come up with a new Truth about herself and what she deserved and what was possible for her in her life, and she had a way to evaluate her options and make choice based on what felt right to *her*.

Instead of, "I am a helpless victim who has given up everything in order to be taken care of," Sally chose, "I am in charge of my own life, and I deserve to do what makes ME feel happy!"

Profoundly light-hearted strategies for unsticking stuck stuff

THE 8 MASTER KEYS TO HEALING WHAT HURTS

NOTES

_____

_____

_____

_____

_____

_____

_____

_____

_____

_____

_____

_____

_____

_____

_____

11
BE WEALTH

The TRUTH about Me

I UNDERSTAND the TRUTH about me
I AM of value! I AM worthy!
I deserve to trust, love & believe in myself

Sensitivity

Sensitivity

INTENTION

My pain & anger
are trying to tell me
something!

INTENTION

My spirit's been
caged and
I deserve better!

Sensitivity

Sensitivity

EVIDENCE of the Truth in my life

This is my Blueprint! This is Who I Am! This is where I Stand!
(Ex.: I play My music, I hold Sacred Space for my clients....)

7 – Evidence:

Think of examples in your life that show times that you have always been living from this belief deep inside.

Wealth-Being

We all want to be wealthy and happy. We think we want more-better: more money, more-better things, more-better love, better looks. We start from the premise that we don't have enough now, and we want more. Or we think that we aren't enough, and it is our fault. We focus our efforts on working harder to get more-better. If I DO more then I will BE more and I can finally HAVE more.

Some of us feel daunted by this effort. Underneath our bravado, we think that we probably don't deserve more-better. Or that we should be helping other people, and not be so selfish and ungrateful. Some of us just give up and settle.

> What if we start with the idea that we are good as
> gold already, and we just don't realize it yet?

According to the Universal Law of Attraction, we magnetize to ourselves what we are. So all we need is to learn how to see and BE the wealth we already ARE. I call that Wealth-Being. To ilustrate the idea, here is a story realting good metaphor about Wealth-Being:

In 1957 in Bangkok, a group of monks from a monastery had to relocate their massive, ten and a half foot tall, 2.5 ton clay Buddha from their temple to a new location to make way for a new highway being built through the city. They used a crane to lift the idol, but it began to crack, and then rain began to fall. The head monk was concerned about damage to the sacred Buddha, and he decided to lower the statue down to the ground and cover it with a large canvas tarp to protect it from the rain.

Later that evening, the monk went to check on the Buddha. He shined a flashlight under the tarp, and noticed a gleam reflected through a crack in the clay. Wondering about what he saw, he got a chisel and hammer, and began to chip away at the clay. The gleam turned out to be gold, and many hours later the monk found himself face to face with an extraordinary, huge solid gold Buddha.

Historians believe that several hundred years before this, the Burmese army was about to invade Thailand, then called Siam. The monks covered their precious statue with an 8 inch layer of clay to disguise its value. Very likely the Burmese slaughtered all the Siamese monks, and the secret of the statue's golden essence remained intact until that day in 1957.

We are all like the golden Buddha, in some way. We are covered with a protective layer, often so well covered that we have forgotten how to remember our true value.

❋ ❋ ❋

```
7 > ° v ° ^ i> ' ° v °    } ° ° >  > V ° i>   ] °
     i° ^ °   °  ° > V  >  °^i i^] °
          °7   / ¶ °
```

What would it feel like to just go ahead and BE our wealth??

And to know that it has been here *in us* all along?

The wonderful thing about going through this process and discovering the Truth about you is that when you look back over your life, you can see evidence of it forever. You have always been this good.

I found a picture of myself in fourth grade, ten years old, smiling out from the photo. It is the same smile I have now! But when I look at my child self, I feel a mix of emotions. In that picture I have no idea what is coming. I wish I could go back there and be a wise guardian angel for myself, offering a deeper truth along the way.

A deeper truth

In fact, that *is* a strategy I often use with people, inviting them to construct, in imagination, from real or invented sources (is there a difference??) a wise advisor or fairy godmother or guardian angel or loving aunt/grandmother figure to be there for the child self for love, hugs, advice, support, and as a truth teller. As young people, we needed to know a deeper truth about ourselves. If we had, it would have made all the difference.

It is not too late to know that now! And to take that knowing now back to then. Time and memory are much less "fixed" than we think they are.

The truth has always been there. We are just remembering.
When I was a brand new mother, I came across an image that fairly rose up from a page in a book about new ways to think of parenting. I felt that this image came to me as a teacher. It has been there in me ever since, and it has seen me through a lot more than mothering.

The image was an acknowledgement of how challenging it is to be a mother, and this wise counsel: to be perpetually aware of the perfect baby under all that poop. The golden Buddha under all that clay... Here is a thought for when we forget:

Have you ever wished your life had a "search function?"

That you could just enter what you are looking for, like you do on the computer, whether it is a lost item or a lost possibility, and just as on Google, all kind of options would show up right there in front of you to be explored?

Well, take heart. We *do* have such a function in our brains.
It is just that we have it set to look for all the possible disasters, mis-steps, scary things, everything that could go wrong or befall us. We have it set for what we have missed out on in life. And consequently,

unbeknownst to us, this very default setting is what is preventing us from accessing the good stuff. Our 'Personal Google' is extremely efficient and unerring. You have sadness playing out a lot in your life? You get mad easily? That delightful man or lovely woman or good job or self esteem keeps slipping out of your life?

Very likely somewhere inside your brain there is a default setting for these eventualities. Fortunately:

Your Personal Search Function *can* be reprogrammed!

You already know that on your computer, the more precisely you choose the words to enter into Google, the better Google works for you to find what you want. Your brain works (sort of) the same way. Everything depends on what you tell yourself.

```
7 > i i °   ° i °   ^i v ° ^°   i] °V   i^ °   i °                    °
```

You need to enter a new and different type of information into your own personal Google—and then sit back and wait for it to trot off, like the well trained beast it is, and bring back what you are looking for.

Our brains really do work like this.

Every living being is curious. Notice how you feel inside when there is something you REALLY want to know. Your whole being seems to go into Search and Find mode, being curious, looking forward, with eager anticipation, intense interest. Think of your dog or cat when you are getting their food ready, how focused they are on what is about to come. It is a feeling of something interesting and exciting going on. It is irresistible!

All life seems to have a focus of seeking-to-find. We depend on this emotion to stay alive. But it is not only for survival, it is the essence of fun and joy. Interestingly, scientists used to call this circuit in the brain the "pleasure center." The reasoning was that since the main neurotransmitter that was associated with the seeking circuit was dopamine, then dopamine must be the "pleasure" chemical.

Dopamine is involved in a lot of drug addictions. Cocaine and nicotine and any stimulant raises the dopamine level in the brain, so scientists assumed that since drugs made you "feel good," people get addicted to them.

Newer research is showing that the drug actually stimulates the seeking center in the brain, not the pleasure center.

Also, the part of the brain that is firing when the seeking is going on, stops firing when the food (or the answer) is found. So...

```
7 > ° i° i>    °   i° ^° i°   t°°
```

Whether it is a search on the Internet or a garage sale, or for a new idea or the solution to an intensely important question, the hunt is what keeps us going.

For a moment, think back to the image of the tiger in the cage. There is nothing quite so intense as the image of a tiger on the hunt, every hair alight with fiery concentration, eyes burning with intense interest. It is survival, but it must be profoundly fun for the tiger too! All that capacity is still there in the caged tiger, but it has been so suppressed that it has been all but forgotten.

```
   °     °  >  °   ^°   i ^i°v ii  }° v°  °>  `°
  i i^ °> `°>   V « >    °>  `°V   ^   ° ^°  i°
       >V  > `>  } > }i° v° i°^   °°
     ° ^°v `> i >    °   °i°> i     °°
```

If only we had known this, back when all those things were happening in our lives. If only we had known how to set our course

by THIS feeling, instead of the need to keep ourselves safe.
We can remember how, now!

Appreciative Inquiry

I witnessed a good example of this recently. I was in a meeting
where we were studying a process called Appreciative Inquiry (AI),
a philosophy of change for individuals, groups, businesses and even
communities, that focuses on what is working, rather than on what
the problems are.

The idea of AI is to train our awareness toward our moments of
excellence, our periods of competence, times when we have felt
most alive and energized, so our attention and intention work like a
magnet to attract more of the same. What is "bad," out of sync, or not
working just seems to begin to fall away.

(More info: appreciativeinquiry.cwru.edu/intro/vision.cfm)

Our group was paired up to ask each other to tell about a specific
time when things were working well, and to talk about what we did
that created a good outcome. I asked my partner the question: "Tell
about a time when you asked the universe for help, and the response
came in an unexpected but perfect way."

It turned out that Karin had just that afternoon met with someone
whose authoritative and controlling manner she usually is
intimidated by, and their interactions have often
ended up with her being reduced to tears. But this time she was able
to change the dynamics between them.

I asked, "What did you do that worked?"
She said she had
decided beforehand how she would be.

And kept reminding herself all the way through their discussion to re-center, and remember her intentions. Her answer to my question came out almost like a poem:

- ❋ I took action on my own behalf quickly
- ❋ I stayed true to my vision, my belief in the potential for collaboration between both of us
- ❋ I stayed in my heart
- ❋ I stayed grounded
- ❋ I reframed my fear so I could see the gift in the situation
- ❋ I stayed in my power
- ❋ I gave myself permission to HAVE power
- ❋ I felt the gift
- ❋ I felt the support of the universe
- ❋ I wasn't a victim

What great tapping phrases these statements would make!

EFT to change the default settings

We really can change the default setting on our programming. That is exactly why we use EFT, the Emotional Freedom Techniques.

For instance, use EFT to change this:

Even though I have this repeating program in my life, because of those events that happened and the people who causedthem, and it is making me mad and sad a lot...

To this:

I now know there is goodness in me, and there has *always* been goodness in me—so I am making these other, better choices in my life now, and I am curious about how that starts happening, sometimes in surprising and unpredictable ways.

Then add:

...and now I choose to ...take action on my own behalf, quickly, or

...and now I choose to ...reframe my fear so that I can see the gift in the situation.

Make up your own!

Am I going crazy?

Here is a story of someone who discovered a capacity that was native to her, and that she could have been using, but just didn't know how.

Many of us have wondered what we would have done in a situation like 9/11. When the second building was struck and the tower next to it was burning, how could people know what to do? There was a time of chaos and turmoil, and then the loudspeakers reported: "All is well now in this building. You can return to your desks."

Many people did return to their offices. It is so awful to think about that now. There is in us such a strong tendency to follow orders, go with the prevailing tide, to assume that the authorities must know what they are doing. (Of course, sometime they do!)

The day after the attacks, I worked on the phone with a young American woman in Belgium. She had just graduated from high school a few months before, and she had wanted to take a half step before jumping into the deep end of going to college. She went to live with a Belgian family to repeat the last year of high school there, having no way of knowing that as a shy, sensitive girl, she was actually casting herself into the middle of the ocean on a tiny life raft in a profound time of world change.

Virtually since her arrival in Belgium a few weeks earlier she had been panicking, she felt like she was going crazy, she felt lost and alone and alien. She was calling her parents, crying, begging to come home.

Her parents, dismayed, were encouraging her to try to stay. And she was getting lots of letters, calls and email from people saying, "You can *do* this. I did it. It was the best experience of my life! Be strong!" All this input made her feel even worse—she thought to herself: "I should be able to do this. I'm letting everybody down. I am so immature. I am failing. I am so ashamed."

We had already had three phone sessions, mostly focused on being able to make good choices for herself, so that she could create an environment that felt good to her and that she could be comfortable in. She said that what she wanted was for people to say they were proud of her, and she admitted to feeling that "other people know what is best for me."

I wanted her to know that it was possible for her to make these decisions, even the one to come home, without framing herself as a failure. As we talked and tapped on those beliefs, I began to work a bit with the story about the people on the stairs, their indecision. To go back, or to stay? How do you know what is right for you? How do you learn to trust yourself? Where in your body does trust live?

We went along in this vein, and then suddenly I said, " What if immaturity is actually letting *other* people decide what is best for *you*? Look what happened to those people on the stairs who went back to their desks."

```
" 7 >  ° v ° >      ° ^ ° > L   ° L i } ° > L i °  ° > i °
   i° V  V i ^ ° >  ° > i° }  ° v  °  ] °  ° >  i °
            >  ° >   i ° i ^ i ° ^ >  ^ ¶ » ° °
```

I heard her gasp all the way over there in Belgium. She said, "I never looked at it like that!" (I have heard other versions of this so often: "I didn't know I could decide for myself. I didn't even know that I wasn't doing that.")

I don't think like anyone else

I asked her to imagine that she could float back over the timeline of her life, looking and sensing for other ties in her life when, in fact, she *had* decided for herself. She was thoughtful for a long time before she began to talk again. But when she did, she began to paint an image of herself of a young woman who knew that she did not think the way everyone else did.

❋ She recognized herself as someone who had always made decisions from a deeper place.

❋ She knew when something didn't feel right to her.

❋ She had very strong ethical, political and philosophical convictions.

Even though she was also a very sensitive, quiet, rather timid appearing person, this young woman was now beginning to touch consciously into the truth of her being, the core of strength and spirit at her center.

```
" V i°  ^i°"  >} > °  ^ ^»  °> i°>V  > i'] °
     }°V > °^ «° i° i>  «  ^ ^°
              ° i°L  iv
```

In her book *Plan B: Further Thoughts on Faith*, Anne Lamott tells the amazing story of David Roche, pastor of the Church of 80% Sincerity. (What a wonderful name for a church!!) David has what he calls a "facial deformity," which came from being born with a huge tumor on the bottom of his face. It was removed, but so was most of the bottom of his face.

He gives talks where he stands smiling in front of the audience for awhile so people can just look at him, and then he suggests that someone ask him, "David, what happened to your face?"

As he responds, he talks about how people with deformities have their "shadow on the outside."

It took him a long time to realize that people turn away not because of what he looks like but because of their ***own fears*** about what marks them as unlovable.

He describes his face as "an elaborately disguised gift from God."

> To find the value in himself, he had to
> really really **challenge all the beliefs** around
> us that if you look good, you will be
> happy and successful.

He preaches being as good and as kind and as compassionate as you can, eighty percent of the time, trusting that you can demonstrate goodness ten seconds here and ten seconds there, and we should be glad of that and savor it when it does happen, because it lets us know that the goodness is actually there inside.

Anne Lamott describes hearing him talk in church, and speaking to the children who are sitting up front. The children get him right away, especially the adolescents, she says in her funny, insightful way, because "to be in adolescence is, for most of us, to be facially deformed."

She says, "David makes you want to help him build a fort under the table with blankets, because it looks like such fun when he does it. He builds the fort, and then lets you lift the blankets and peek in, at him and at you. You laugh with recognition, with relief that your baggage and flaws are not vile, unmentionable. It's like soul aerobics."

She quotes David Roche: "I've been forced to find my inner beauty. Doing that gave me a deep faith in myself. Eighty per cent of the time. And that faith has been a window, so I can see the beauty in you, too. The light in your eyes. Your warmth. So thank you."

LEILA

Thankfully, I have matured to the point where I don't have to act out my pain anymore. My hormones have settled down into middle age and I have found the 12 Step program, and 'energy psychology,' which through gentle tapping on some of the acupuncture meridians has calmed me considerably, and brought about a miraculous lowering of my pain.

The best shift that happened while I was talking to you came when you were able to coax me to say out loud "I am of value." And then even "I am of great value!!" I was surprised by how sure of that I was—the sureness came from deep inside—and I am certain that it is a result of the EFT work I have done over the last few months— especially gently rubbing over my heart and saying "I deeply and completely love and except myself."

I have discovered that the love I so desperately needed is already within me, and that a higher power has been holding me all along.

✻ ✻ ✻

I love the butterfly metamorphosis story told by Elisabet Sahtouris in Chapter 10, because it teaches us that the Truth of us has been within us all the time. The butterfly is not an alien or different organism developing within the caterpillar. The caterpillar/butterfly is a *single organism*, with the same genetic code. The butterfly capacity is always there within the caterpillar, and the metamorphosis happens in perfect timing.

NOW: Add all this evidence into your tapping affirmations!

✻ ✻ ✻

NOTES

12
BE **SELF**-ISH

The TRUTH about Me
I UNDERSTAND the TRUTH about me
I AM of value! I AM worthy!
I deserve to trust, love & believe in myself

DIRECTION
I know
I *can* choose
Yum!

BEING
SELF-ISH
I do what I LOVE!

Sensitivity

Sensitivity

♥

♥

INTENTION
My pain & anger
are trying to tell me
something!

INTENTION
My spirit's been
caged and
I deserve better!

Sensitivity

Sensitivity

EVIDENCE of the Truth in my life
This is my Blueprint! This is Who I Am! This is where I Stand!
(Ex.: I play My music, I hold Sacred Space for my clients....)

8—Direction:
LIVE HAPPILY... EVER AFTER!

8 – Direction you are pointing yourself in.
How does it make you feel to think and act this way?
Living by the Principle of Yum and Yuck!

8 – Self:
Be SELF-ish!
Care for your Soul.
It is your way of healing the Soul of the Earth.

❋ ❋ ❋

There is a one-paragraph story by Kafka in which a cat chases a mouse down a long hall. The walls are narrowing, narrowing—the walls of any nightmare—until at last they meet and the mouse is trapped.

"It's not fair!" the mouse cries. "There was nowhere else to go!"

"All you had to do was change directions," the cat says.

And then he eats the mouse.

❋ ❋ ❋

New decisions

You have completed the Map, gone through the process of discovering the deeper truth in you, and you have found that, *in fact*, this is who you have always been.

Now you are in a profoundly powerful inner place—you can set your own course through your life. You can be your best self. You can point yourself in the direction that feels best to *you*.

However, most of us have not yet learned how to make these decisions. Faced with choices, we don't know how to choose.

In this practical chapter I will share some of my most favorite, fun, interesting, effective strategies for knowing how to choose.

You will discover:

* ❋ how to experience the choices in your body
* ❋ two ways to experience the choices intuitively
* ❋ a deep and profoundly useful meditation
* ❋ that each of these strategies creates clever and insightful tapping phrases!

Underlying everything I say in this chapter
(and in this book!) is my passionate exhortation to you to
BE SELF-ISH!

We have all grown up with people around us who pounded it in to us—maybe even literally: "Don't get a big head!" "Don't be selfish!" "You only think of yourself!"

Now is the time to reframe this idea. I spell Self-ish with a BIG capital S and a hyphen between Self and "ish."

Think of "Self" as standing for your Soul,
the best and brightest in you.

Self-ish means "caring for your soul."

If you don't take good care of it, your soul will starve. It will become caged. You will suffer. This is a universal law.

```
9  °  1 -/°V > i°v  °   °  ^    t°°
      ° ^°  i°  °      it
```

When you truly care for your soul you are caring for the best and brightest in *all* of life—because at that level we are all droplets in the same unity. At the level of individuality, we are soul energy appearing as us. If you only care for others, *you* get left out. And you feel left out. Don't you?

```
    >   }°v  °    °^   ° i>  ^°`  }°
        °  >  °}  i^°  ^i°  °   °>  `°
           i°>  `°v ii`  °   °
```

Think of the direction you want to go toward. What internal question gets you going there? It is different for everyone. For me personally, good questions are:

❋ How could I do this in a fun and interesting way?

❋ Does this make my heart sing?

❋ How could I reframe and expand the meaning of this to make it interesting and meaningful to me?

❋ What is the positive intention that is trying to emerge here?

It is pretty simple, really. It all comes down to Yum and Yuck. You do the Yum things, and avoid the Yuck ones. Or if you have to do a Yuck thing, try to do it in a Yum way.

I first heard about what I think of as the Principle of Yum and Yuck from Sarah.

SARAH

YUM and YUCK

Sarah asks herself: Is there something that I am meant to learn through having fibromyalgia and chronic fatigue?

Her answer to herself:

For me it is about learning the lesson, finding the gift, finding out how my body is doing the right thing for my highest goal. This is about coping with my temperament, recasting my understanding of my life, the Me that I really am.

My biggest outcome is that I have been turned back into my true nature, the voice of my spirit. I am training myself to hear my own inner voice. I am thinking of Yeats' poem, "We come from God trailing clouds of glory…" Or what it says in the Bible, "Be still and know that I am God."

(When Sarah said that, I suddenly had a new, deeper sense of what that phrase can mean. I had always assumed it meant sort of, "Be quiet, now. Just know that I am God and everything is OK." What I was hearing now was this: Stillness IS God—meaning an inner stillness in us, even a stillness in motion.)

Before, I was on a roller coaster all day long, in my thoughts, trying to accomplish things all day long. Now, my life is NOT full of people.

The thing I worry about is that I am not doing enough to change my old habits. I am trying to move forward, not drift. Are there things I need to do differently? How can I support myself to do what I need to do? What do I need to do?

I have the powerful feeling that I need to meditate, to sit for half an hour, and be still. But I have such a strong resistance to that.

(I asked Sarah "How else might you 'be still and know that you are God' besides meditation?")

Well, I remember the oncologist O. Carl Simonton saying that life boils down to yum or yuck. So my goal would be to have a clear resonance inside to tell me, "Is this a Yum or a Yuck?" Hey, I am getting a Yum response just to saying this!!!

I realize that if somebody has been traumatized, you don't think you get to ever have Yum.

You are not allowed to have happy feelings.

Or you don't deserve them.

You flail around trying to figure out the right thing to do so you don't get yelled at.

Where do you feel Yum in your body?
It's a happy fluttery feeling in my chest. Whee!!!

What about Yuck? Where is that?
Hmmmm. It' s a flat, unhappy feeling. An "I never do anything right" feeling.

So where in your body do you get that flat unhappy feeling?
Well, my spirit feels inadequate. Forlorn.

How do you know? That would have to be a feeling in your body, through your senses, as well as a thought.

Mmmm, maybe my chest is tight? No, I feel like I am making that up.

My guess is that the Yuck feeling is Sarah's inner response to an alarm signal, arising from past experiences, to dissociate from her body. It is her body's response to painful experiences. She has cut herself off from those painful feelings.

The body is still feeling the emotion, and she is behaving and acting now from that sense of flat, unhappy, inadequate, forlorn, never-do-anything-right-ness, but her conscious awareness of it has been blocked. So it seems to her in the moment that "Yuck is Just The Way Things Are."

Sarah realizes that she feels like she **should** meditate in order to get to a place of feeling better. (Her statement, "I need to meditate," was my clue.)

So now she wants instead, or maybe in addition, to learn to recognize the feeling inside of Yuck. Often it is her body's unconscious response to a "should," which is almost always accompanied by that feeling of resistance.

And then she could look for what would be a Yum. Asking herself, "How can I get the feeling of inner stillness, and God, and Yum?"

Her "assignment" is to pay attention to her body's response to Yuck, so that she can learn to recognize the signal and seek out Yum ways of getting what she wants, instead

Refined Yum

Later Sarah sent me this email:

I have a little refinement for "yum"—it has a feeling that I call the "Girl Scout at camp feeling"—I recognized it when I planted a little tree in my yard and put wood chips around it. I felt a little up-rushing feeling of sweet - sweetness? Joy? Happiness?

```
   ° ^ ° > ° v ii  } ° v ° i   ^  i ° > } V ° >  ˎ °  ° ^ °
          i ] ° i ° ^ L  i °
```

It is even hard to talk about because it is so special. This is a feeling I had at camp, in the woods, as a child in Girl Scouts. I fell in love with the part of my yard that I got the feeling from.

Then the other thing I have noticed is, I need to preface tapping with the announcement to myself that it is not intended to short circuit any process my body, mind, spirit et cetera is going through, but is intended only to give **creativity and support for the natural and true processes that are taking place.** It is not that the tapping may not shorten the process; it is that it will do so by providing creativity and support, not by cutting it short artificially.

This makes all the difference for me. I can tap whole heartedly, and I feel that the things I tap for are at the heart of wanting my heart's desire and clearing the way for work and service that feels like inner snow-boarding.

HOW TO BE SELF-ISH

1. Find Yum and Yuck in your body

❋ Begin by sitting quietly for just a moment, with your eyes closed.

❋ Notice what happens inside when you say, "The world is an unfriendly place."

❋ Pay attention to thoughts, images that come up, and especially pay attention to how your body feels. Do you get tense? Where specifically in your body do you feel this question? What happens to your breathing?

❋ Now shift your position (*when you change your position you change your mind*) and take some deep breaths.

❋ Say inside, "The world is a friendly place." Again, notice thoughts, images, and especially notice, very specifically, what happens in your body. Where do you feel this statement? What happens to your breathing?

❋ Think of some of the experiences that irritate you or leave a bad taste in your mouth. (Don't do major traumas here.) Again, notice where and how you experience these very different states of being in your body.

❋ Shift your position.

✳ Think of some of your very favorite or peak experiences. They can be big or little, it doesn't matter. What counts is noticing how you felt at the time, *in your body*.

✳ Say the word NO, and feel it inside. Again, notice where and how you experience this word in your body.

✳ Shift your position.

✳ Do the same for the word YES.

✳ Take a moment to gather all the impressions that your body has given you. Sort them into Yum and Yuck.

Now you have a fail-safe way to make choices about what is right for you from the inside out.

One note to pay attention to:
I have found that, for many people, the only way they have known how to say YES to themselves is by saying NO to what was in their environment. So when they first try this exercise, the feeling for "yes" is actually the feeling for "no." This can be very confusing at first.

Pay close attention to your inner experience when you do this exercise. Make sure you recognize this reversal, and get a *real* actual bona fide YES in your body. You, especially, deserve YUM!

✳ ✳ ✳

2. Finding Intuitive Answers #1
adapted from the work of Nancy Rosanoff

Think of a problem or a situation for which you would like an answer or insight.

Look around your home or office, and choose:

An object or space that you like
Something that you don't like or are dissatisfied with
Something new
An animal

Look at the answers you wrote down, and consider what you have learned about yourself in the light of these suggestions from your intuition:

❊ The object you like represents an *overview of what you would like to have happen.* Think about the qualities of the object you chose and how it relates to your question.

❊ The thing that you don't like represents **what is blocking the situation.** Think about how your object might represent barriers to your problem.

❊ The "something new" represents *the answer.* Look closely at this object and how it came to be in your space for clues about how to solve your problem.

❊ The animal represents *new behavior* that you may need to adopt in order to achieve the outcome you want.

Now, how can you incorporate what you have learned from your intuition into tapping set-up statements?

3. Finding Intuitive Answers #2

Think of a choice you have to make between two different options, items, or possibilities.

In your imagination, create a box for each of the choices.

❋ For each box, pay attention to what comes to mind for size, shape, the materials it is made of, how the box opens (if it does), is it wrapped or not, is it suspended in space or resting on a surface, and whatever else you can think of.

Now, imagine that you come upon both boxes side by side. Which one are you drawn to?

❋ What have you learned about your intuitive choice from this exercise?

How can you incorporate your insights into tapping set-up statements?

4. How to be SELF-ish

Steve Jobs, inventor of the MacIntosh computer and its mother company Apple, has probably never done these exercises, but he is really good at following his intuition!

Have you ever read his Commencement address to the students of Stanford University in 2005? It is reprinted all over the Internet, but Apple turned down my request to reprint it for you here (even though I am a Mac user!).

It is called '*You've Got to Find What You Love,*' originally printed in the *Stanford Report*, June 14, 2005. I recommend that you read the whole thing, at
news-service.stanford.edu/news/2005/june15/jobs-061505.html

In the meantime here are the highlights. Jobs begins:

"I am honored to be with you today at your commencement from one of the finest universities in the world. I never graduated from college. Truth be told, this is the closest I've ever gotten to a college graduation.

"Today I want to tell you three stories from my life. That's it. No big deal. Just three stories.

"**The first story is about connecting the dots.**"

He talks about dropping out of college but continuing to hang out on campus, checking out whatever he found interesting. Among the many apparently impractical things he did, following his curiosity and intuition, Jobs was drawn to take a class in calligraphy: "It was beautiful, historical, artistically subtle in a way that science can't capture, and I found it fascinating."

Ten years later he built that appreciation for design into the first Mac computer—the first computer with beautiful typography.

"If I had never dropped out, I would have never dropped in on this calligraphy class, and personal computers might not have the wonderful typography that they do. Of course it was impossible to connect the dots looking forward when I was in college. But it was very, very clear looking backwards ten years later."

Again: **you can't connect the dots looking forward; you can only connect them looking backwards.** So you have to trust that the dots will somehow connect in your future. You have to trust in something—your gut, destiny, life, karma, whatever. This approach has never let me down, and it has made all the difference in my life.

His second story is about love and loss.

He describes beginning Apple in his garage, working hard for ten years to build it into what became a $2 billion company, and then getting fired from his own company. He spent several months feeling like a very public failure. But slowly it began to dawn on him that he still loved computers and inventing:

THE 8 MASTER KEYS TO HEALING WHAT HURTS

"I had been rejected, but I was still in love. And so I decided to start over.

"I didn't see it then, but it turned out that getting fired from Apple was the best thing that could have ever happened to me.

"The heaviness of being successful was replaced by the lightness of being a beginner again, less sure about everything. It freed me to enter one of the most creative periods of my life."

During the next five years, he started two very successful new companies, fell in love, got married and started a family, and developed an incredible line of new technology that is now the essence of Apple's current expansion.

"I'm pretty sure none of this would have happened if I hadn't been fired from Apple. It was awful tasting medicine, but I guess the patient needed it. Sometimes life hits you in the head with a brick. Don't lose faith."

> "I'm convinced that the only thing that kept me going was that I loved what I did."

You've got to find what you love. And that is as true for your work as it is for your lovers.

Your work is going to fill a large part of your life, and the only way to be truly satisfied is to do what you believe is great work. And the only way to do great work is to love what you do. If you haven't found it yet, keep looking. Don't settle. As with all matters of the heart, you'll know when you find it. And, like any great relationship, it just gets better and better as the years roll on. So keep looking until you find it. Don't settle.

His third story is about death.

"When I was 17, I read a quote that went something like: "If you live each day as if it was your last, someday you'll most certainly be right." It made an impression on me, and since then, for the past 33 years, I have looked in the mirror every morning and asked myself:

" v° '> ° i i° i° > ^ °'> ° v ° ° v i]° ' ° °
> ° ° ' ° > ° °> °>L ° ° ' ° '> ¶ » °

"And whenever the answer has been "No" for too many days in a row, I know I need to change something.

"Remembering that I'll be dead soon is the most important tool I've ever encountered to help me make the big choices in life. Because almost everything—all external expectations, all pride, all fear of embarrassment or failure—these things just fall away in the face of death, leaving only what is truly important. Remembering that you are going to die is the best way I know to avoid the trap of thinking you have something to lose."

"9 °> i°> i> ' ° > i' °/ i i° ^° ° i>^ ° °
°v ° ° i> »

Jobs describes being diagnosed with incurable pancreatic cancer, and what he learned about Death being "the single best invention of life," that clears out the old to make way for the new. He eventually found that he had a rare form of cancer that was operable, so he survived. But he took a real Yum lesson from this Yuck experience:

"Your time is limited, so don't waste it living someone else's life. Don't be trapped by dogma—which is living with the results of other people's thinking. Don't let the noise of others' opinions drown out your own inner voice. And most important, have the courage to follow your heart and intuition.

"They somehow already know what you truly want to become. Everything else is secondary."

✳ ✳ ✳

Be SELF-ish:

On Meditation

I include these thoughts here in response to a question from Leila, one of the wonderful correspondents whose words from emails are sprinkled throughout this book.

Many sensitive idealists are sensitive to the inner worlds as well as to the overwhelming emotion and stimulation in our daily world. Leila wrote to say that when she meditated she found herself too open to too much information, and it was frightening to her. How could she protect herself, she asked? Should she just shut down?

I offered Leila a mini version of a meditation that was the subject of an online class taught by David Spangler (Lorian.org). He suggested that one might begin the meditation by creating a safe and familiar inner space, like a room filled with favorite objects that also hold personal spiritual significance and power. Include in the visualization a doorway that opens out onto a porch that looks over a lawn or garden, and a road in the near distance.

The porch acts as a personal boundary, and you can invite and place a guardian there: a tree, an animal, an angel, or whatever comes into your imagination as a guardian of the boundary of your own personal, sovereign space. When you open into meditation, you remain in your room or on your porch, and any other source of information is required to remain on the road unless you invite it to approach closer. **You are in charge of your space.**

David described the value of this set-up this way:

This is a meditation that will help you to create an energy field that can act as both an invitation for a larger perspective to arise within you, and a vessel to hold that perspective.

This exercise is based on the fact that we are all—each of us—already and always in contact with a variety of inner sources. That we don't experience this consciously is generally a good thing—how much information can you integrate on a daily basis anyway? How much can you use? So there is a wisdom and intelligence involved here on the part of our larger Self.

But much of this information is underneath the threshold of normal recognition. If we are not quiet enough within ourselves, not still enough, we won't be able to register it.

It is also stimulating, since information is also energy, and it can move us in different directions where we may not wish to go. That is, it can cause incoherency and a lack of inner integration and centeredness. Think how scattered you can feel when you are in a noisy room in which several people are all vying for your attention at once, and pulling on your sleeves to have you move in their direction and pay attention to them.

So, at the very least, to open to a deeper level of perception, we need silence and stillness, we need to have a good and strong sense of ourselves so our coherency is not lost, and we need to have a plan for what we're going to do to integrate the information so that it is useful to us and not just part of mental and emotional clutter. And we need a way to drain off excess energy that we cannot assimilate or use.

Finally, you want a way to close the door and say no to stop a flow of energy or information that threatens to overwhelm you or when you sense that you are finished or have reached the end of your energy in the moment.

"DO NOT OPEN"

Often we use phrases like, "I'm going to open to the inner worlds," or "I'm going to open up to the information I need," or "I need to be more open."

We understand what we mean by this, but the words can convey an image to our unconscious that is not what we want.

THE 8 MASTER KEYS TO HEALING WHAT HURTS

```
/ i i ° ^ ° > ° ` v v i i V i ° L i  i i °
L i  } ° i V i «   i ° >  ` ° L i  } ° « i °
```

"Being open" may suggest a boundary-less state. Simply being open in the sense of having no boundaries can leave us vulnerable to being overwhelmed.

Instead, we are going to use the image of going to the periphery of our being where we can be receptive to new information and vision, but still be within boundaries that protect us and give us an integrative structure.

Look at it this way. When a cell wants to interact with its environment, it doesn't split open its cell membrane and let the environment simply flow in. It doesn't rupture its differentiation and protection as provided by the cell wall. Instead it modifies or adjusts the cell wall in a manner that makes it more sensitive to and engaged with its immediate environment.

So, we go to the edge, to the boundary, but not beyond it. We are receptive, alert, and aware, but not simply "open."

Create an inner state of mind
in which you are peaceful, attentive, and receptive, while
remaining within the boundaries and protection of
your own self
and your own spirit guardianship.

Within this receptive space, information can arise in some form. It could be a feeling, it could be words, it could be images, it could be something else.

```
* > ° > i   ] ° ^ ] ° L ° ` ° ° ^ > ° °
```

Profoundly light-hearted strategies for unsticking stuck stuff

Know that you can "send back" or close yourself off to any information you do not choose to receive.

9   °> i° °V > }i° ii °°

Your inner allies, all inner allies, honor the sacred in you as the sacred is in them. They ask that you stand strong and tall and confident in who you are. No inner ally of any kind, from any "where," that is aligned with your truth will ever talk down to you or criticize you or tell you to do anything.

(Text from "Inner Lens," online class by David Spangler, reprinted with permission)

All of the true sources of inner wisdom want us to be as fully and completely and radiantly and brilliantly who we most deeply are. We are meant to be standing strong in who we are, saying with our entire being, "This is Where I Stand."

Only then can we, as highly attuned sensitives, be useful vessels for what we receive, and for what we offer, both into the world and into the inner realms. The inner realms receive from us as much as we receive from them.

Care and attention to our lives and to all life at this deep level is truly what is meant by "Be SELF-ish."

❋ ❋ ❋

A Recap:
At the very least, to open to a deeper level of perception, we need silence and stillness, and we need to have:

❋ **a good and strong sense of ourselves** so our coherency
   is not lost

THE 8 MASTER KEYS TO HEALING WHAT HURTS

❊ **a plan for what we're going to do to integrate** the information so that it is useful to us and not just part of mental and emotional clutter

❊ **a way to drain off excess energy** that we cannot assimilate or use.

❊ **a way to close the door** and say no to stop a flow of energy or information that threatens to overwhelm you or when you sense that you are finished or have reached the end of your energy in the moment.

The bud
stands for all things
even for those things that don't flower,
for everything flowers of self blessing;
though sometimes it is necessary
to reteach a thing its loveliness
to put a hand on the brow
of the flower
and retell it in words and in touch,
it is lovely
until it flowers again from within, of self blessing.

from St. Francis and the Sow,
by Galway Kinnell

Profoundly light-hearted strategies for unsticking stuck stuff

NOTES

13
THE (ENLIGHTENED) MEDICAL VIEW OF CHRONIC PAIN

Chronic pain:

※ Can have a syndrome diagnosis

※ Can be a complex central nervous system pain disorder

※ Abnormal brain activity starts with a trigger, does not return to normal

※ This brain response may be adaptive for protection

Thankfully there is an increasing number of people in medical science who are showing interest and skill in alternative and complementary approaches to understanding health and wellness. Here are some ideas from three of them.

First there is some information on the body's chakra system from **Dr. Christiane Northrup**; and some fascinating ideas on childhood experiences, beliefs and illness from **Dr. Dietrich Klinghardt**. I have included their websites with an invitation to you to delve further.

I also include the transcript of a talk given by **Dr. Nancy Selfridge**,

Chief of the Complementary Medicine and Integrative Wellness
Clinic in Madison, Wisconsin during a presentation we made together
at the Association for Comprehensive Energy Psychology Conference
in 2005.

The ideas are much the same as she expressed in the Foreword of
this book, but here she is speaking informally to energy psychology
practitioners. She shares more about her personal thoughts and
experiences. I like that in a doctor!

❊ ❊ ❊

CHRISTIANE NORTHRUP, M.D.

On her (very informative) website, Dr. Christiane Northrup says:

The location of a disease within the body—where it occurs—has
spiritual, psychological, and emotional meaning and significance.
Just as spirituality is free-flowing and ever-changing, our body's
energy system is always changing, and the potential for healing or
disease is present at all times.

She describes the body's chakra system, the energy centers that
connect our neurological and endocrine systems with our emotional
and psychological issues. In this view, common to Eastern cultures
and the practice of acupuncture and Traditional Chinese Medicine,
the chakras mediate energy flow between the physical and the
emotional body.

When we accept this perspective, Dr. Northrup says, we can get a
sense of how cultural and personal wounding may have spiritual,
psychological or emotional consequences that can set us up for
subsequent health problems.

She suggests that fibromyalgia and many other chronic conditions have their basis in the first chakra, found at the base of the spine. She describes the first chakra as having to do with the immune system.

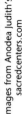
images from Anodea Judith's sacredcenters.com

The immune system has the job of maintaining our identity as a physical being in the world. It identifies what is "me" and what is "not me," and makes the distinction clear through its response.

She says that **the first chakra, therefore, has to do with our sense of safety/security in the world:** knowing when to trust or mistrust, knowing when to feel fear and when not to. It tries to regulate the balance between independence and dependence.

Other physical issues that show up in relation to the first chakra, according to Dr. Northrup, are those having to do with physical body support, like the hip joints, and the spine.

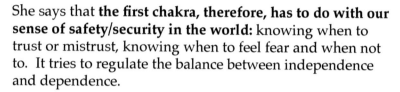

Our spine is all about our support in the world. So chronic back problems are found in the first chakra column, as well as conditions like scoliosis, sciatica, arthritis, auto-immune diseases, skin problems, rectal tumors/cancer, blood problems, and chronic fatigue.

Read much more on her website: DrNorthrup.com

DIETRICH KLINGHARDT, M.D., PhD.

A very interesting perspective on the relationship between childhood experiences, beliefs, and physical illness comes from neurobiologist Dietrich Klinghardt, M.D., PhD.

In 1997, Dr. Klinghardt delivered a talk to the American Association of Orthopaedic Medicine titled, *"Psychological Factors in Chronic Pain: An Introduction to Psychosomatic Pain Management."*

He begins by referring to British neurologist and researcher Barry Wyke, who has shown how the neurological signal from a painful stimulus travels from the receptors at the injury site to the thalamus, where the message is split: one pathway goes up to the sensory cortex, telling the patient where the pain is, and what particular sensation it causes (warm, pulling, pressing etc.).

The other pathway goes to the frontal lobe, which is part of the limbic system, which, among other duties, is the holder of our unconscious responses to stimuli. ***Stimulation of neo-cortex area gives the patient the emotional experience that goes along with having pain*** ("it makes me sick, hopeless…I feel terrible…I am afraid…, etc.).

Klinghardt asks

"Why are we putting all of our attention on using such invasive procedures to 'fix' pain, rather than treating the emotional part of chronic pain? It is the emotional suffering that makes pain so uncomfortable. All that fearful self talk about how it is bad now and it is going to get worse, maybe it will never get better, will I be able to take it, it's my fault, maybe I deserve this anyway… Why aren't we helping people deal with their pain at this level?"

He cites a 1992 study by the San Francisco Spine Institute published in *Spine Magazine* (Vol 17, #6, pp 138-144, 1992):

"100 adults with MRI-proven severe lumbar disc herniations were preoperatively interviewed regarding five possible traumatic situations in their respective childhood:

* Physical abuse
* Sexual abuse
* Emotional neglect/abandonment

THE 8 MASTER KEYS TO HEALING WHAT HURTS

✳ Loss of one or both parents (divorce, death etc.)

✳ Drug abuse at home (alcohol, prescription drugs etc.)

The study concluded that **"the result of surgery and post-operative pain have little to do with the surgical procedure itself but largely depend on factors that date back to the childhood of the patient.** It can be easily extrapolated from this study that the same is true for many or all of the other procedures used in pain management…"

Dr. Klinghardt is a strong supporter of EFT and other energy psychology techniques as a powerful resource for what he calls "uncoupling techniques:"

"When a conflict from childhood is uncovered, a new intra-cerebral neuronal connection is made from the limbic system to the cortex. The patient becomes more 'conscious.' The conflict-induced electrical energy from areas in the limbic system can now flow to the cortex instead of constantly arousing areas in the hypothalamus. This energy becomes a source of greater vitality and clarity.

"However, the pathway from the conflict to the hypothalamus is habituated and needs to be uncoupled ('de-conditioned')."

Dr. Klinghardt has an interesting way to look at how experiences and beliefs affect disease and healing. He describes five levels of healing in a way that I, with no medical training, find almost comprehensible and very evocative, using an example of how different healing methodologies at each level impact a patient who is suffering from anorexia nervosa. You can find the complete article, and many others, on his website: NeuralTherapy.com/

✳ In his model, the lowest level is the *physical body*, the foundation upon which everything else rests. We experience it through our senses. It is our connection to the earth and the source of our physical energy. It ends at the skin.

✳ The second level is the *electromagnetic-body* or "body-electric."

Profoundly light-hearted strategies for unsticking stuck stuff

It is the summation of all electric and magnetic events caused by the neuronal activity of the nervous system. "Theoretically," he says, "these bio-magnetic fields extend into infinity."

❋ The third level is the *mental body.*

❋ The next level is what he calls the *"dream body."*

❋ And the "highest" level is what he calls the *"spirit body"* (he is not seeing the different levels as corresponding to more or less valuable) .

A case of anorexia nervosa

Klinghardt offers this fascinating look at how true healing works. He relates the hypothetical case of a young woman who has the clinical diagnosis of anorexia nervosa, saying that true healing requires simultaneous work on all five of healing levels.

❋ Oh the first level, the physical body, she is likely to have a **clinical zinc deficiency**. He says that since the laws that govern this level are the laws of biochemistry and mechanics, if you keep her on a life-time of zinc supplements, she would probably stay reasonably well.

❋ Looking at this patient at the next higher level, the electro-magnetic body, we may find that she has a "hidden **mal-absorption syndrome** caused by over-activity of the sympathetic celiac plexus (which leads to vasoconstriction of the absorbing lymphatics and blood vessels in the gut)."

This condition may respond well to periodic treatment with acupuncture. The patient would start absorbing zinc from the food again and would improve without zinc-supplements.

This shows that the second level has an organizing effect on the first level.

❋ At the third level, the "mental body," this young woman may

Profoundly light-hearted strategies for unsticking stuck stuff

have an **unresolved conflict** with her father, who was very oppressive during her childhood—stern, punishing, critical and at times violent. Klinghardt says that "the unresolved memory held in her limbic system is responsible for stimulating the hypothalamus and sending sympathetic stress messages to the celiac ganglion, which is now in a pathological state of chronic arousal."

This conflict can be resolved by some kinds of counseling, especially energy psychology. Then, "the celiac ganglion cools permanently off and the patient starts to absorb zinc again—and gets well!"

The third level has an organizing effect on the two levels "below" it. Also, now that the patient is absorbing her food better and her nervous system is functioning better, she is more able to do the emotional healing work. He keeps emphasizing how the levels support and nourish each other.

❋ Doing the healing work in the fourth and fifth levels, what Dr. Klinghardt calls the **dream body** and the **spirit body**, involve understanding the effect on this young woman of her family's ancestral belief system (see Chapter 7 in this book).

Calling upon his knowledge of German psychologist, Bert Hellinger's **Family Constellation Systems**, Dr Klinghardt describes it in this way:

The typical family-constellation in a young woman with anorexia looks like this: invisible to anyone on the outside, including the children in the family, the patient's father was deeply rejected by the mother—his wife—and subtly pushed her out of the family.

The patient in turn is unconsciously loyal to the rejected father and holds the "magical belief" that if she disappears, the father would stay. "I leave for you" is the operative sentence and a sign of a deep and strong love and loyalty for the father.

° °   i > ° ^ ° > ° > °v ° i°V i ° °ˋ^> « « i>   °

The father's oppressive behavior (behavior belongs to the third level) was his way of responding to the wife's rejection of him (which in turn triggered and re-stimulated *his* unresolved childhood issues).

Healing on this level often leads to instant disappearance of the associated unresolved conflicts on the third level, and—in this case—disappearance of the celiac ganglion dysfunction and therefore improved zinc absorption.

Again, the energy required for this healing work has to flow upward from the lower energy supplying levels. Simple interventions on the lower 3 levels would be laying the foundation to make the work on the fourth level possible.

❋ What about the fifth level, the "spirit body"? Healing at this level, Dr. Klinghardt says, involves understanding, acceptance and forgiveness, both of **other** and of **self**, and "doing something good with the newly gained hope and vitality and clarity." He says that if the work is not done on this level of the spirit, there may be a gradual relapse of the condition.

In my opinion, Energy Psychology techniques like **EFT can work towards healing on all of these levels.**

❋ ❋ ❋

(From O. Carl Simonton, MD is a pioneer in holistic health and founder and medical director of Simonton Cancer Center in California, and author of "Getting Well Again" (1978) and "The Healing Journey" (1992).)

❋ ❋ ❋

14
ENERGY PSYCHOLOGY

Perspective on Pain

Repeated experiences of stress or trauma can cause the energy system to become disrupted and the flow of life force restricted, limiting our access to our capacity to think and act and make choices.

Chronic pain is a stress or trauma-related depression, obstruction, or interruption in a particularly sensitive person's electrical system.

Acupuncture...

... is the grandmother of EFT.

Here is some wisdom from its 5,000-year history about treating pain as disharmony in a person's energy field.

Much of it I have learned from notes taken by my daughter during her training to become a doctor of Traditional Chinese Medicine. The particular class that offered this information was taught by an extraordinarily wise teacher, Sharon Weizenbaum.

Her clinic and school's website is WhitePineHealingArts.com/clinic.

The Physical Being

The physical level is considered by Chinese medicine to be mostly concerned with aches and pains of the muscles and bones.

It can be the first and last level affected in a disease process.

```
V V  ` }°  °    i^i° i`V >  °  i  ]°
  «   ^ V >  °«>   ° ^°V >  ^i`°L  °L  V  ^°
       °  i° i ` >  °V >  i^ °
```

Therefore, aiding the movement of qi (chi, vital energy) along the meridian pathway can relieve pain.

Physical problems can arise from an emotional or spiritual source. For example, a person who has carried a lot of responsibility from an early age might feel as though there were a large weight on her or his back, causing chronic tension in the neck and shoulder muscles.

Emancipating the energy lodged within those muscles not only relieves the physical discomfort, but also releases the emotional and spiritual blocks that are integrated with it.

❋ ❋ ❋

The Emotional Being

There are seven main emotions considered in Chinese medicine: anger, joy, worry, pensiveness, sadness, fear, and shock. These seven emotions are viewed as broad categories containing many other types of feelings.

Each emotion has a particular effect on the movement of qi within the body, and each emotion is related to a certain organ. The liver is most influenced by the emotion of anger, for example. Emotions that are out of balance can compromise the energy of particular internal organs over time by disrupting the flow of energy through the meridian pathway that supplies those organs or body systems:

* Shock suspends energy
* Worry ties it up in knots
* Fear directs qi to descend, temporarily suspending a person's connection with his or her energy.

Emotions can lead to disease when they are experienced for a long period of time, when they are particularly intense, go unacknowledged, or are suppressed.

For example, if a person experiences a lot of anger and does not express it, over time, qi can become constrained, which can lead to headaches, aches and pains, tiredness, and anxiety.

Treating the Spirit

Acupuncture regards fibromyalgia, and possibly most chronic emotional and physical pain, as "shen disturbance," or "shen disharmony."

Shen is spirit, the "knowing-how," the intelligence that knows how to grow us from a zygote to an adult, or an acorn into an oak tree. On a physical level it is the knowing-how to run our bodies; on the emotional level it is a knowing-how to respond to life and move in life appropriately. Spiritually, it is a knowing-how to move in the direction that feels right for our destiny.

Shen is rooted in the heart.

In a Shen disturbance, we lose our connection to the "knowing-how" in one of these areas. Shen will flow where the attention goes, because we are in partnership with spirit and it responds to our attention. If we think obsessively, it will go from our bodies to our heads, and we will feel scattered. Shen will always want to root deep within our bodies, and it will ask us to bring it there through our signs and symptoms.

If someone gets angry at us, our attention goes out away from our bodies. Living in fear in an abusive relationship forces our attention out of our bodies. Alternatively, if we are not allowed to talk, our energy turns in on itself.

✳ The experience begins as a physical feeling.

✳ It becomes an emotion when we identify ourselves with the feeling, and tell ourselves a story about it.

✳ People will say they felt tired and heavy, and then they realize they are "depressed."

```
7 >  ° i°V >  °>  °i    ° ^° i>   °>  °i i }i V °
   «  V i^^°  > ° ^°}  }° ° ° i°L '
```

In Traditional Chinese Medicine, when our sense of reality gets affected, it is called an emotion because it is affecting the Shen of the heart.

Signs that the energy imbalance is on a spirit level:

✳ Flat expression

✳ Manic expression

✳ Disheveled appearance

✳ Inappropriate behavior, dress, hygiene

✳ Unable to make eye contact or staring intensely

✳ Language used: "I can't do that…" "Nothing has ever worked," they don't want to "do anything

People with this appearance have lost their connection to their sense of possibility, a key attribute of the spirit.

Blown fuses

Repressed anger and grief is at the basis of much chronic pain and depression. Following is Ananger Sivyer, a practitioner of Traditional Chinese Medicine from England, talking about her understanding of how this works.

Anger Management & The Meridian System

by Ananga Sivyer
The Association for Meridian Therapies • TheAMT.com

The meridian system as I understand it operates as an interface between the physical and more subtle energy channels of the body.

It operates very much like an electrical circuitry, and it can be "blown" as can a fuse. As with fuses, this is a protection device and, again as with fuses, if not repaired, areas of that circuitry governed by that particular fuse will remain "offline."

Let's clarify that a bit further so that we can be fully aware of the significance and ramifications of this for us, as human beings. I have a toaster in my kitchen that is a little sensitive, and every so often it lets out a spark and trips the fuse in our fuse box.

When that happens there is no toast in our house, there are no lights in half the kitchen either, until somebody goes to the cupboard and flips the switch back. The toaster is on a circuit that also affects the kitchen lights; there are two basic resources on that circuit. But that means the socket that the toaster is plugged into is affected too, so no using the blender either, or the microwave.

Profoundly light-hearted strategies for unsticking stuck stuff

THE 8 MASTER KEYS TO HEALING WHAT HURTS

Now, if we generalize that basic understanding over to the meridian system, we can quickly understand that if a particular 'circuit' blows due to shock, trauma, or overload, then the resources of that circuit are also affected. This happens to varying degrees, as the meridian system is more subtle and complex than the wiring in our homes, but nonetheless the principle remains the same. We have energy circuits, those circuits facilitate certain experiences and nurture specific resources, and if they are disrupted then those resources will be directly affected.

```
/ i° i ' > ^°^i i° > ^° i}  >   ^]°
   «  iV  ^°> '°v>V   >   ^ °
```

One of them is even referred to as 'the heart protector,' and its main purpose is just that, to protect the heart.

```
  ^°  i° i>  ° ^°  i°   }° v° i°  i}°     ]
     °  ^ °L i° «  iV i'° > ° >  °V ^ ^°
```

The heart is the master fuse and if that blows, logically enough, the whole system goes offline.

The twelve main meridians are each teamed with a physical organ in the body, and that organ is responsible for a key set of emotions and experiences. Here balance is the key, and EFT is certainly an incredibly easy and effective tool to apply in this regard.

According to the Traditional Chinese model of health, anger has its place, even rage, but these emotions are considered to have a time and place in which they are useful and appropriate and, after their purpose has been achieved, they should fade and take their place in waiting until called again, if genuinely required.

When a fuse blows in the circuits that generate the experience of anger, a strange loop can develop whereby that anger is re-generated repeatedly, and for matters of trivial concern. It can become a self-perpetuating cycle and, unless it is interrupted and restored, it will soon begin to burn out other areas of the circuitry.

If, in a system that is operating under extreme pressure, anger gets the job done, or more significantly, feeds back to us a sense that it protects us from certain unwanted situations or experiences, it can become an overused and dominant emotion.

When that happens the scales of balance are tipped and the resources at the other end of that scale go offline.

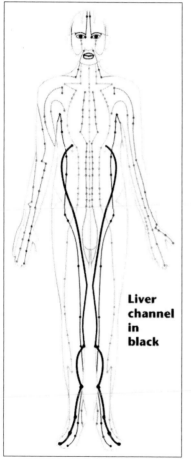

Liver channel in black

Meridians Most Relevant To Anger

Let's look at the organ meridian channels that are relevant to anger: There are two, and they work as a team with the liver and the gallbladder.

The liver is responsible for an assortment of emotional expressions, with anger being the most prominent. The governing of patience comes under the control of the liver and its partner the gall bladder—impatience is regarded as a sign of imbalance within this team.

When disturbed, the liver energy reacts with aggression and shouting, or with depression, and also with crying of a particular type: this crying is the kind born of sheer frustration and is likened to a safety valve.

❊ When the liver energy is disturbed we shout, and when we shout, we disturb the liver energy.

❊ Frustration disturbs the liver energy, and frustration is a manifestation of disturbed liver energy.

Here we have the loop-effect, a self-perpetuating cycle. This is an area that I consider to be of key importance to any of us interested in how we might operate more smoothly.

A genuine smile

There is an exercise in the systems of Chinese Energy medicine called "smiling at your inner organs."

We tend, in the West, to view such things as cultural quaintness. The Chinese smile at their inner organs, how nice, what an interesting custom. But there is practical purpose here, very simple and very effective. It is a practical exercise in personal care and kindness. When I was a child, I would have given anything, truly anything, to receive a smile from my father instead of a shout. A warm, genuine smile is a thing that is greatly soothing to the spirit. So there is a purpose here—paying (and in using that word, I mean really *paying,* as in actively investing) attention to our internal organs and energy systems with a few moments of gentleness, kindness and soft appreciation actually does go a long way to keeping our circuitry free from blow-out.
OK, so that's nice to know, a preventative measure and something to try in the milder cases of irritation; but when you're really mad, will it work?

Sadly, probably not. There are times when you could tell me to smile at my liver and I will do so gladly, and laugh too; but there are other times when you would really wish you hadn't said that!

It's all a question of time, place and circumstance. Remedies fit the occasion: we don't stick plasters on gaping wounds, and we won't benefit from a spell of inner smiling when there's a blown circuit.

Remembering to tap....

But we can often tap, someway, somehow. If we can train ourselves to use EFT at such times, even if it is as simple as making a habit of raising a hand and tapping the side of our eye when we feel that rage bubbling to the surface, we have a very good chance at developing some excellent anger management skills. And not just that, but resource reclamation, too.

I mentioned balance within the meridian system. This means a point of stillness between two ends of a possible range of experiences; a place where we have all the emotions, responses and actions available to us along that scale.

A balanced liver will show itself in impetus and forward momentum, which includes aspirations and higher ideals. and it facilitates achievement without aggression. It has the energy of springtime and is a generator of new growth and beginnings. It is creative, nourishing and forward moving.

What the liver really dislikes is frustration, those times when you feel you are really trying and getting nowhere. And if you get a few of those in a run, or over a period of time, the liver gets very irritable.

Here's an overview of some of the resources available to us when the liver energy is balanced:

Drive, planning, impetus to start projects, endurance, good reflexes, perseverance, quick and clear intellect, an agreeable disposition, ambition, patience and a sense of general well being.

Anger can even be a facilitator

In an appropriate expression accompanied by clear thinking and a genuine desire for a beneficial outcome, controlled, useful anger

Profoundly light-hearted strategies for unsticking stuck stuff

is available when the liver is balanced, and furthermore, it can be turned on and off like a tap!

Untamed!

Now let's look at the other part of the team, the gallbladder. This is where things can get really dangerous! The liver simmers, it resents and shouts and it rails, but **the gall bladder untamed is the generator of pure wrath and fury**. It is the place from which the energy to wreak havoc and destruction comes; and at that point the judgment-making skill of the gall bladder goes offline in order to fully facilitate all hell being let loose most efficiently.

The gall bladder, when balanced, facilitates good decision making abilities, creative impetus and inspiration. When imbalanced or blown, it will manifest to varying degrees: irritability, rage, pure reckless wrath and fury, bitterness, constant sadness and impertinence.

Anger Management - Furious Old Ladies

Here's a (case) that I cannot resist mentioning. I will keep it brief here, but will mention that I really learned some amazing energy-system-impacting-the-physicality associations from this.

A very small, sweet, elderly lady once came to see me about pain in her shoulder. As she was talking she became agitated and said that there were things held in her about which she felt very bitter.

We chose her a set-up statement and began to tap the sequence of EFT points. As we reached the gall bladder point at the side of her eye I noticed a slight shift in her and so we continued tapping on that point for a few seconds longer. What happened next I truly wish could have been captured on a camera. It is one of the most amazing things I've seen!

That lady's face—that had previously looked so gentle—turned into a mask of pure rage. It was actually scary to see, it was like a horror movie where you see a face begin to turn into a monster—there was a twisted and distorted expression of hatred and fury that was very real and very frightening.

Gradually, as we continued tapping, her face relaxed until, after a few moments, she sighed and said, "Thank you, dear, that does feel much better." Bloody hell! After she left I had to go and stand outside for a few minutes to compute that one.

And there have been others too.

I remember one lady who was furious with her husband for dying and leaving her. Her left shoulder was frozen and barely moveable, and when she left it was moving much more freely.

(Energy Psychology trainer and author) Silvia Hartmann has mentioned that she got relief by tapping her middle finger point.

This is the heart protector, as previously mentioned. It is the meridian that governs the extreme of our emotional response, and when pacified it facilitates an awareness of, and concern for, the wellbeing and feelings of those around us.

> Silvia says, "There is no shame in having a blown-out, unstable major body meridian as a result of accident or incident. I didn't do this to myself, and I wasn't 'born bad'."

We wouldn't leave a fuse tripped-out in our homes, and neither should we suffer such havoc in our real home—the physical and energy body that strives to serve and facilitate us always.

(reprinted with permission)

NOTES

15
A SPIRITUAL PERSPECTIVE ON PAIN

Chronic pain is a "disharmony of spirit" reflected as pain in the body

Restricting the expression of our deepest truth results in anger, fear, and sadness. These feelings are messages from the body, life pain experienced as physical pain.

We may become constricted protectively around our own pain in the belief that: "I can't express what I really feel. In order to feel I have control over what happens to me, and in order to justify taking care of myself and doing things that help me to grow spiritually... I (unconsciously) believe that I must remain ill."

When I first met Nancy Selfridge, and we began to talk about fibromyalgia, she said, "Doctors don't know what to do with their fibro patients. Physicians hate to be unsuccessful, and they are almost always unsuccessful when they try to heal chronic pain with conventional medicine."

Even if chronic pain is puzzling to medical science, it makes perfect *spiritual* sense.

Modern psychology, science, and spirituality are converging upon the understanding that we are what we believe.

```
/ i °  >  ° i °  ^ i i ° i °   ` ° >  ` °    i ^ «  ` °    °   °
>  ` ° > V  °   °   ° > ^ ° i i   } °  ° ` °   °   >  °
i °  i « i V  ] ° >  ` °    ° i °   v i i ° > L   °   >   ° ° °
```

Our human lives make visible, personally and globally, the dramatic interaction between the universal forces of expansion and constriction.

❋ In personal terms, the effects of the forces of constriction show up in our emotions as rigid thinking, fear, worry, anger, shame, lack of self-esteem, our sense of un-worth.

❋ In our bodies, the effects show up as pain.

We struggle with feelings of not-enoughness. The idea of worth is tied closely to the idea of *self*, how we define and identify self, and to the idea of the *Sacred,* and how we define and identify the Sacred.

The Dalai Lama has expressed astonishment to discover how widespread the feelings of unworthiness are in the Western world. It would make sense that in a philosophy like Buddhism, in which the self does not exist as a permanent, unchanging thing, but rather is a flowing process at best and an illusion at worst, the idea of worthiness would not make a lot of sense.

What or where, after all, is the self that could feel worth or unworth? Hence the Dalai Lama's puzzlement.

But in the West, the self is a very important concept, and thus its "worth" or "unworth" *is* something to which we pay a lot of attention. This is particularly true if we believe in a religious teaching (and in a God) that says that we have to earn our way into heaven— and that not everyone is going to do that! I believe that the devilish problem of self worth in our lives that haunts us at every step is in fact an angel/ally/teacher in disguise.

A feeling of unworthiness doesn't just "go away." We can't take a pill to make it go away, or have surgery to cut it out. We are not going to get rid of it.

```
    7 i°  ^ °   i > }i°   ^i  i^°  °
\°   °^i^i°v°    °'vvii  ]°^ °  > °  °
    i>  ^° ^  i   }°'vvii
```

❊ ❊ ❊

Spirituality, Pain
and the Trance of Unworthiness

Tara Brach begins her book, *Radical Acceptance*, with this poem from Wendell Berry:

'The Trance of Unworthiness'

You will be walking some night . . .

It will be clear to you suddenly

that you were about to escape,

and that you are guilty: you misread

the complex instructions, you are not

a member, you lost your card

or never had one . . .

Wendell Berry

Whatever happens to us as children that is less than we deserve seems to end up in a simmering pot of beliefs that could be labeled "helpless, hopeless, worthless."

I suspect, though, that we are all in this together—we are all doing our bit to heal this pattern in the human psyche. And that, whatever else we are doing with our lives, this is one of the purposes for our being here.

What makes us think
in this limited way about ourselves?

Our entire lives are shaped by living the questions that arise from our struggle toward gaining an inner knowing that "I am enough."

This issue of feeling like we need to "measure up" is like the grain of sand in the oyster shell of the human consciousness. It keeps coming up, and we keep returning to it, mulling it over, working it, deeper and deeper, so that eventually we will get to some truth about it.

I believe that each of us is doing this on behalf of all of us. The individual insights and transformations and healing that each of us accomplishes helps to clear the way for the larger being of humanity.

BARB

Barb talked about feeling insecure *again*, critical of herself and despairing to have these feelings surface when she thought our previous work had cleared it all.

"I am constantly feeling like I'm not as good as everyone else," she said. "Like I don't measure up."

We had an interesting discussion about the phrase "measure up."

* ❋ Who was doing the measuring?
* ❋ Where was "up"?
* ❋ Who got to decide how UP you have to be before you measure up?
* ❋ And what did "measure up" mean to her?

For her, we discovered, it meant "interacting as comfortably as other people appear to." Some of her beliefs around this were "I want to interact—but I am scared to, I don't know how to, I feel backwards when I do." She felt this as a tense, gripped, on-guard feeling in her stomach.

I mentioned German poet Rainer Maria Rilke's response to a young admirer who had obviously made a similar comment:

"Have patience with everything that remains unsolved in your heart. Try to love the questions themselves, like locked rooms and like books written in a foreign language.

"Do not now look for the answers. They cannot now be given to you because you could not live them. It is a question of experiencing everything.

"At present you need to live the question. Perhaps you will gradually, without even noticing it, find yourself experiencing the answer, some distant day."

Rainer Maria Rilke
from Letters to a Young Poet

So what might be the questions she could be asking inside that would "live her toward the answer?"

First, she offered this question: "Why do I feel like I don't measure up?" I said I thought a "why" question like this usually just produced a lot of critical mental response.

Eventually we came up with these questions to live:

- How will I know when I am interacting comfortably?
- What do I need to do to feel like I can interact comfortably?
- To what do I want to measure up?
- How might I measure?

We talked about how we think there is a standard of "perfect" that we are supposed to measure up to, a standard that in fact we never get to. We considered the thought that, possibly, perfection lies in "doing the best I can, right now, this moment."

ANAIAH

I thought of my daughter (now in her twenties, working in marketing for a financial services company in Boston), and how hard it had been for her to learn tap dancing.

Anaiah was in second grade. Her two teachers at school were of the "old school." They had their traditional way of doing things. They were nice people, but any child who didn't fit into the system that they had developed over the years was seen as kind of defective to a degree.

It didn't help that Anaiah's older sister had passed with some ease through their class a few years earlier. Anaiah was an intuitive, very sensitive, perceptive child, bright, warm, generous, funny. Kind of like a fish in water—unconscious of her life, not able to step back and observe what is happening and think about it. She was *in* it.

Back then she always had a hard time with sequential tasks, language. As an adult now she is a wonderful writer because she has learned to write from her heart. But at that time, much about school made her mad and frustrated. She was very much the perfectionist.

If what she did for her homework wasn't perfect, she ripped it up in a rage.

A very visual learner, often she didn't understand the teacher's spoken directions. If she could *see* what she had to do, she would understand, unless the work called for abstract thinking. Abstract ideas, explained in language (which is itself abstract), fried her mind. She learned best when there was an analogy with something she understood, something real from her own experience.

That year in school made her scared to death.

How many of us have had this happen? She came to lose trust in herself. She was afraid to take risks, afraid of making mistakes, had to get what she did perfect. She easily fell into a rage or into despair, and shut down. The sound of the slamming bedroom door punctuated our lives on a regular basis.

That spring of second grade Anaiah took the tap dance class. Tap was not really her style. She had been good the year before in a free-flowing, interpretive dance class where she had even caught the attention of the teacher. But this year there wasn't going to be anyone in that class that she knew, and that was too scary for her. She did know a girl who was going to take the tap class, so even though tap wasn't really her style, she took tap for the safety of having someone in there that she knew.

She found it very difficult. Tap is like language. There is a set pattern, it is sequential, precise, and fast. She had a young, enthusiastic dance teacher, who talked very fast. For Anaiah, the class was confusing right from the start.

A few weeks into it, whenever Anaiah would "mess up" she began a pattern of falling into a heap in the middle of the floor, in tears, un-rousable by fellow students or teacher. Someone trying to help her would make her close off even further.

This happened every time the class met. I sat on the floor outside in the hall reading—sometimes I would watch through the crack in the door, anguish in my heart. Sometimes she would come crying to me.

After weeks of this, I asked her if she wanted to quit the class. It seemed to be torture for her. Why not let it go and find something more fun, more nourishing? She always said no.

But it got worse. Eventually the spring recital began to loom in everybody's mind. It was far enough away yet, but still I had horrible visions of Anaiah up on stage, falling apart in the middle of the piece—there were only four girls in her class, so it would have been pretty obvious—or refusing to participate to begin with, hard in another way.

I cast about for a way of unraveling Anaiah's knotted-up mind. I asked her what was stopping her from leaving such an obviously painful experience. "I would be a failure, " she said. Quitting for her meant failing. This situation would be hard enough at any time, but now it was especially challenging since she was so sensitive about her ability to succeed already, set up by the performance anxiety produced for her in school.

I said, "So succeeding is really important to you." Tearful nods.

I told her about how she learns.

I explained that the way the teacher taught was not how *she* learned. *I wanted her to understand that the issue wasn't her ability as a dancer.*

When the teacher talked so fast and so much, Anaiah's brain froze and shut down, and then her body couldn't do the movements. When people came to try to pull her back into the class, meaning well, it drove her deeper inside herself, away from the painful experience.

I told her, "You're seeing it the wrong way. Quitting the class won't make you a failure. Actually you fail when you back off, when you collapse and refuse to participate. What you want is success.

"So do this:

"See each class as an opportunity to practice being successful at sticking it out. Take the energy you were using to keep yourself protected from the hurt of failing, and use it as strength and power to push through the bad feelings, *to help you get through the class, every time. There* is your success."

Because Anaiah thinks in big pictures, big concepts, she has a tendency, under stress, to take a detail—a single incident of "messing up"—and make it be everything, her definition of her entire self worth. This puts a frame around every misstep, a frame that says "failure." This frame caged her, locked her up, kept her from getting out there to her big goal of succeeding.

I offered her a different perspective:

❋ Keep your big goal the same. Succeeding is a good state to be moving toward.

❋ Now, organize the details, in this case each class, as a way of keeping track of what you want.

This way, you are constantly cycling back and forth between your big picture and the details, making sure that they are all in the same frame, and that the frame is one you like, one that feels good to you.

Anaiah thought she could do this. It deeply touched my heart to watch her teaching herself to get though each class. She found that she could "mess up" *and* go on. She couldn't do it easily, but she could do it. As the weeks went by she became more and more confident in her ability to succeed in the face of failure. To have "failure" and "success" happening at the same time.

❋ I wanted her to change what she meant when she said those words to herself, so that she was thinking of herself as successful, even while things were not going well. ❋

Profoundly light-hearted strategies for unsticking stuck stuff

The day of the recital was huge for both of us. There she was up on stage with her classmates, tapping away, grinning from ear to ear. That grin didn't leave her face, even as she made missteps. She did pretty well, in fact.

And there I was in the front row taking pictures, tears pouring from my eyes, my heart bursting with pride and love. And relief. I cry all over again, remembering.

What sustains a particular thought or feeling like, "I am unworthy"?

Why does it persist within us? There is something at work here. Something is keeping that thought and feeling alive and present within us. What *is* that?

I think that it is possible that there is an energy within the psychic environment of our Western culture (and perhaps to one degree or another in other cultures as well) that promotes a mental-emotional-spiritual condition which a person may experience as "unworthiness"— if there is anything in a person's history or personality pattern that would resonate with the effects of abuse, woundedness, ineptness, then that person may be more vulnerable to taking on the energy pattern of unworthiness.

It is not that *all* feelings of unworthiness are the result of our being "taken over" by forces or energies in the environment. But our own personal feelings can be exaggerated and exacerbated by such a collectively-held and experienced energy.

```
7 > i i ° ° L i  i i °  °     ° > L    °  ^ i v °
      ° L i ° >   >  V >  ° i v  V i ` °
        L °  ° i « i  i V i ^ ° °
```

If I am prone to feeling a lack of self-worth, then there are plenty of sources in our culture that can reinforce that tendency. But there are also forces that reinforce the opposite, so if I am feeling good about myself, I can find reflection of that as well.

```
 / i˚i i } ˚ v ˚          i ^ ^ ˚         ^ ˚ >  ˚ i i } ˚ v ˚
      ' ^V   iV      ˚    >  ' ˚ ^  >          ˚
```

It is a sense of alienation and separateness. It disempowers and disconnects us from some of the natural forces of creativity that are within us.

When I imagine going into this energy pattern to experience it deeply, it feels as if I have landed at the feet of a great, giant beast which, while not evil or negative in itself, is so profoundly impersonal that   it could easily crush me without ever knowing I was there.

I feel as if I have stepped into an inhuman place, and that if I just went with the flow of this place, I would end up a stone, inert, passive, isolated.

This sounds dramatic, but there are forces like that in our world, vast forces whose function is to crystallize, particularize, and condense, keep things in stasis.

These forces are at the other end of the spectrum from the forces that generate creativity, growth, change, even chaos. The growth of all life requires a balance of both of these forces. Personally, I believe that our own individual lives are about finding the balance within us. It is not easy! This is not new news.

CONFLICTING INTENTIONS

I am reminded of a lovely session I had with a woman who had had a truly magical experience a few years ago. While she was traveling in another country, she met a man who seemed to be her soul

Profoundly light-hearted strategies for unsticking stuck stuff

mate. They have had a long distance relationship for a long time, but it now seems increasingly impossible to maintain or develop this relationship further. Neither can leave to join the other in the foreseeable future.

She was feeling wrenchingly torn between "keeping him," and "letting him go." When we really looked deeply into these two apparently conflicting flows of energy in her, it turned out that the positive intention in her of keeping him was actually about having someone in her life who deeply "gets" who she is, appreciates her, loves her unconditionally. That made it possible for her to feel worthy, validated, and free to be who she is, with all choices and possibilities open.

On the other hand, the part of her that wanted to let him go had the positive intention of wanting her to be free to build another relationship to which she could really commit, so she would be able to share a life with a companion she could love and be loved by. That would lead to true fulfillment, she felt.

She began to see the similarities between these two positive intentions. She could sense that they weren't really in such deep conflict.

Both of them wanted her to feel free to be who she was, happy and fulfilled, from the inside out, not dependent on the opinion of someone else.

As she moved with this realization she began to say things like, " I get it! I am who I am. I need not have these conflicts. I am *all* possibilities—in *me*.

"The light inside me is self-validating. It is already there— it doesn't need another person to put it there."

"I can allow it to be there, and let it come out in my expression of being me. In the long run it doesn't really matter what I do about this relationship."

It was a moving moment. She looked transformed.

I just read an article about her in our local newspaper the other day. She was featured as a successful business-woman who had left her old job that she disliked, to take the risk of creating a new business doing something that she loved.

There is a quality of energy or presence that each of us carries within us throughout our lives. That energy, as it expresses through us in ways unique to each of us, has the capacity to form empowering, nourishing, co-creative, and liberating connections, actions, creations.

As humans, I see us as open flowing systems, capable of drawing in and transforming energy from the infinite into the particular. Our actions and our choices form our individual bodies and lives.

However, the fact is that we often hold within ourselves smaller "systems" of energy that are more closed than open. These systems diminish the open flow of energy in us, and the overall effect is to make us feel more isolated, separated, alienated from the cosmos around us.

When we have a wound, a memory, a rigid habit, a restrictive belief, it is as if we constrict ourselves around it. Like the grain of sand in an oyster, these "particles" of ourselves are knots of energy where we have become less flowing, less open, more self-protective—or even self-denying. In the very act of living each day, we run into situations that can cause such constrictions.

But suppose we are constricted about ourselves?

Suppose the very idea of being a self, of being a unique person—of being a person at all—is seen as a condition of separation and constriction?

Suppose I feel, for instance, shame at being a human being, or at deserving to take up space in the world; or suppose that I struggle with having a physical body with its passions, appetites, instincts, fleshiness, etc.

I cease to be as open a system as I might be. The flow of life-energy, of light, of power within me, is diminished. All the other ways I create constriction and obstructions in my life become that much more powerful, that much more difficult to work with.

A person with asthma is familiar with what happens when the chest muscles tighten and the lungs feel constricted during an asthma attack. They can feel that they will never breathe again. An asthma attack might make them feel like they are collapsing into a tight little gasping, wheezing ball.

In the same way, when we feel alienated for some reason from ourselves, or that our "self" is a condition of—or a reason for—constriction, it is like a metaphysical attack of asthma. If this feeling is consistently denied or "stuffed" so we don't have to feel it, it can show up in the body as pain.

Even though it is not possible to fully prove this scientifically yet, **there is ample clinical evidence that the symptoms of any disease in the body can be framed as a response to some kind of inner mental, emotional and spiritual constriction.**

Chronic pain is a perfect example of a "spiritual dis-ease" in the body-mind-spirit system. The symptoms of fibromyalgia, for example, are fatigue, sleep disruption, pain, depression. As Gary Craig, the developer of EFT, said to me once, **"Fibromyalgia is to the body like low self esteem is to the personality."**

Much of our religious heritage implies that the soul is "somewhere else," residing in another realm from that of the body. I believe that the body *is* the soul. I believe that the body is *"distilled soul,"* as it were. Wouldn't it make sense that the fatigue, pain and sadness of chronic pain could be a physical and emotional response to, or maybe a mirror of, the blocked joy, love, and creative expression in us?

```
/ i°  } > ° i>   }° v° i°   ‘°
    "^«   »° ^ L" i>    »°°
```

You could say that the movement of spirit and life throughout the cosmos *is* the breath of God, the respiration—the inspiration—of co-creation.

Ideally, this breath *should* move in us and through us freely.

We are each a lung of the sacred, and we expand and contract so that spirit—the breath of God—moves freely and empoweringly through us to all our world.

```
   7 i°V > ° i>  °  °i > } i   °   ^i i^]°
 ^ii°  ^i i^°> ^°^>V i']°^«   > °L i }^p
          ° °^« i° v]°
      L  °L iV > ^iv °L i }° ii°
```

To incarnate is a divine activity—after all, the cosmos *is* an incarnation—the original one. All other incarnations, manifestations, and expressions of life replicate it.

We can learn to experience ourselves in a way that expands us, and restores us to a feeling of openness and flow.

It doesn't mean we don't still have wounds, challenges, problems, pains, doubts, and all the rest of those feelings and experiences that constrict us, but that these constrictions take place within a larger context of flow—and thus are capable of being healed, transformed, and restored to openness and flow themselves.

Then we can engage and co-create with others in ways that feel right to us. Our actions and choices can carry and assist the power of the flowing energy of the universe itself. This is true healing.

THE 8 MASTER KEYS TO HEALING WHAT HURTS

I believe that chronic pain is a message to our humanity—indeed a cry to the best in us, to say that **we are selling ourselves short!**

People with chronic pain are like the canary in the mine—remember how the old time miners used to send a canary in a cage down into the mine to see if there was enough oxygen down there to support life. If the canary lived, the miners would be sent on down to work. If the canary died, well, I guess it was too bad for the canary…

Perhaps like all illness, chronic pain in our times is a message that our bodies are sending to our conscious awareness:

❊ ❊ ❊ ❊ ❊

Profoundly light-hearted strategies for unsticking stuck stuff

16
SOME
EVER-AFTER WORDS

What about when healing "doesn't work"?

Someone asked me this question recently. It got me to thinking of people with whom I have worked for a long time, who have definitely improved, but who look like they may, for whatever reason, carry the theme of their dis-ease through their lives. All of us who work with healing have thought about this question.

I want to share two stories, both with permission, about people who have been profound teachers for me through their own life process. I feel honored to have been co-creative partners with them. They have not "healed," but they have helped me a lot to reframe for myself what healing *means*.

I continue to learn from both of these women. In both of them, a healing energy is thriving and at work in its own way. They are two women who I admire a lot for their courage and ability to survive immense odds. I feel privileged to be part of their journey. They have certainly been part of mine.

KAT

One client who has been a profound teacher for me is "Kat," with whom I have been working for probably eight years. She is in her early 50's, and has been a prostitute since she was 20.

Kat is the product of an extremely abusive alcoholic home, has that learning style they call disabled and dyslexic (she wasn't able to finish high school), and she was subjected as a teenager and young woman to multiple hospitalizations for mental problems, including several sessions of shock treatment. She has seen many therapists and psychiatrists over the years, sometimes willingly. She has an addictive personality, is an avid member of AA, and is quite familiar with the jail system.

Meeting her in her own world

I have learned so much from working with Kat. As a result of her referrals over the years, I have even developed a minor specialty in working with prostitutes. From the beginning, I got a chance to practice meeting her in her own map of the world. She had stopped seeing a number of counselors who right away wanted to get her to quit her job. This is the only job that Kat has ever had that gives her—in her mind—a sense of her own autonomy, her own ability to make her own way in the world, and I knew that she would be out of here if I did not wholly honor that world view. She says I am the only practitioner in her life who ever has.

The first work we did together (and we did this quite successfully for a long time!) was to help her develop rapport and other similar skills that would make her a better prostitute. That is how I framed it for her, but in my mind I knew that anything that increased her sense of self-esteem was going to be of value to her in the long run. And it has been.

There is so much that I could write about Kat: her bright and curious mind, generous spirit, deep heart, profound compassion, strong survivor instinct. She has changed dramatically over the years that we have worked together. But she has not "healed."

> Over and over and over again I have had to
> redefine what it means to heal.

I have used *everything* I know in working with her, and invented new things as needed. Her favorite tools of our work together are EFT and deep relaxation.

I am not trained as a mental health professional, and so in some ways I have been able to see into Kat without the pre-framing that I might have had with academic training. I believe that she is probably a high functioning person with some mental illness, perhaps schizophrenia. She is truly terrified to leave her work. She is terrified of the future, which is looming rapidly larger because of her age. She literally cannot continue this job much longer. But she has no alternative that she is willing to—or capable of—actually embracing.

I have come to the conclusion that her emotional wounds may be too profound to heal in the sense that she would be able to find mental and emotional balance, get a "real" job and become a "regular person" in the world.   It has been a learning experience to discover this for myself, and to see how our deep healing work together does work, and doesn't work, both.

I am learning about the depths and shadows of healing from watching Kat continue to spiral down and up through the same life lessons over and over again, and return to the same problems over and over again. It could be that someone else would be able to offer Kat more than I have, but I know that I have been instrumental in her life. She tells me that all the time.   And she is an inspiration to me—her ability to hit bottom and keep coming back from it, to the direction of health, at a higher point than she was at before.

An endless healing spiral

I have come to see Kat as moving along a spiral of healing that is endless. She believes, and I think this is likely true, that our relationship is what has kept her alive in the last few years. She is careful, as am I, to maintain a professional relationship between us, but I sense that her regular appointment with me is a literal lifeline for her.

The particular benefit, to her, of our work together
is her clear and grounded knowing, now,
that she has worth and value.

This is something that she never knew. She has now had a long and deep experience of connecting with someone (me) who she trusts, who can see and mirror back to her who she really is. She is not internally strong enough to maintain this knowing in her daily life for long, but now she knows it *is* there and she knows how to access it. Kat is a real illustration of EFT developer Gary Craig's adage about the power of pointing yourself in a *healing direction*.

She has been the source of so much musing in me about healing and life purpose. I have, over the years, been coming to the conclusion that we are asked in a given life to do as much as we can, and we are not held responsible for what we couldn't manage when we were doing our best. (Though no doubt another opportunity will come around again…)

CAMILLA

Another person who has been a challenge in a sort of similar way is Camilla, with whom I have also been working for quite awhile.

Camilla has a degenerative spinal disease, a form of scoliosis. She can't tap on herself physically, so we have found several ways to improvise together. However, every time we come close to something deep, she falls into a kind of unconsciousness/sleep. Frequently she can't be roused enough to go on with the session. But usually we manage to work our way around it.

Camilla is in her 40's, a bright, creative woman, college graduate, who has done a lot of interesting things in her life. She has also had some huge challenges, among them an emotionally abusive family, severe dyslexia, and depression.

She has taken some incredibly brave actions—for instance, as a wheel-chair bound individual, jumping out of an airplane strapped to a parachuting instructor, only to have the parachute tangle and him land on top of her, breaking both of her legs. She does a lot of public work around disability rights, and she is a teacher for a state-wide program that is a kind of basic self esteem training.

We have done lots of deep identity-level work. I have learned about disability, about ability, and about survival. I intuited early-on that the main fuel for most of her life has been anger, anger at her family, insensitive teachers, other children in school, doctors, life itself, and above all, anger at her body. Anger has kept her going.

Camilla hates going down the street in her wheelchair and seeing people who can walk but who don't take care of their bodies. In her mind, if she could only get up and walk, *all* of her problems would be solved. She has spent her life seeking healing. She has gone to all manner of doctors, and does endless work with alternative healers from psychics to energy healers.

I finally realized that healing to her means *being able to walk.* Anything short of this means defeat, failure and low self worth to her. Interestingly, we were able to shift her off of anger as a life force—a huge transformation—but then she found that she had no will to live, no energy for life.

Anger was literally what was keeping her alive.

To me, our work all along—but especially now—is about reframing the meaning to her of having a "dis-abled" body. She has a set-up equation that is going nowhere: She can't love her body because it is disabled.

Therefore she cannot love herself. She understands this, but keeps coming back to the old story, though with less anger than she used to have. I continue to try everything I know how to do with her. We have done lots of psychological reversal work, but it hasn't fully "stuck." Yet.

A tricky balance

One strategy that I have had, and keep returning to in various ways, is helping her to find something that she could do that would use everything she knows, all her experience and wisdom, to share with other people in a way that would give her the kind of sense of worth and purpose and sovereignty that comes from within.

It is tricky, because the Catch-22 of public assistance is that she can't make too much money or she will lose the assistance, and the work that she does won't make her enough to cover all the attendant care she needs. So she can't really develop meaningful life work that supports her.

The other interesting bit here is that if Camilla gives up assistance to live in, say, a nursing or group home, she gives up the quasi-social life complete with ready "friends" that attendant care offers. To say nothing of giving up a lot of attention.

One of the main benefits of our work together for Camilla is that she is now open to and accepting of her spirituality.

She was very cynical and disdainful before. She also now understands how deep her self hatred goes, and how damaging it is. It took a long time for her to admit this. She keeps returning to it, although now she has very different ways to frame her situation that are more life giving.

I have always thought Camilla should teach inner spiritual coping skills to others with disabilities. But she shies away from that because it would mean accepting, in some deep way, her own disability. Accepting that she has this body.

She was talking awhile back about having gone to her physical therapist, who basically told her that no matter what she does, "gravity is winning," and her body is collapsing in on itself as her spine collapses, and there is nothing she can do. Nice work, PT. That reminded her of a doctor many years ago who said something similar, about if she didn't have spine surgery, which had a 50% change of killing her, and would be debilitating in other life-limiting and threatening ways, her spine wouldn't collapse!

In both cases she just gave up. Why struggle? Why bother? Why try to eat healthy, exercise, take care of herself, why live at all?

Searching outside

As she was talking about this I realized I had an image forming in my mind of her spine, S-curving in on itself, and I was thinking about how her life—her issue, her soul dream, if you will—was really focused around "seeking a spine."

All of her life she had been seeking to find her spine *outside herself* in a belief system, a healing modality, a kind of work, a healer or therapist, a love relationship. She was seeking a surrogate spine to make her life worth living.

I started telling her a bit about a weekend training I had done with a group that has studied for many years with philosopher/ spiritual teacher/writer David Spangler in Seattle. We were working with the imagery of a wizard's staff, what it meant symbolically, metaphorically, cosmically, and we did certain exercises with it as a personal spiritual metaphor.

I talked a bit about how we imagined taking this charged image of a powerful personal staff into our own bodies, into our very spine, and experienced it standing there, our own bodies standing as the staff connecting body and soul, earth and heaven, the sacred. I could see the wheels turning in her mind as I talked.

Then I said, "This would be a powerful workshop for people with spine problems! You could teach it! I could help." Suddenly she whirled her wheelchair around to her computer and typed, in big, bold letters:

"THE SPINE WORKSHOP: Create Your Staff of Life."

What a cool idea!

This workshop has so far never actually materialized. Gradually, I became aware that it might not happen unless I took the lead to develop it, and I wasn't able to do that at the time, nor did I feel it was appropriate to do so.

I asked David Spangler about his inner impressions of Camilla, and gained some further insight into why a person might choose not to heal. It was interesting to me that his inner perception corroborated my own intuitive insights, and also correlated with much of what we have learned from our EFT work with serious diseases.

Some of what David said:offline

When reading your descriptions, I had a vivid image of her with her legs cocooned, as if separated from her body, and of an inner voice telling her, "I have no legs, I have no legs." There was a sense of this voice tied to a previous life, though no specifics, but the strong sense was that this condition was a karmic one, something she set up for herself in this life. Actually, the sense was that she is living two lives at once, this one and a previous one, like running a tape loop that has gotten stuck.

The anger that fuels her life seems to me fundamentally self-directed (though of course she turns it outward towards others), but there is also anger at some previous circumstance (that is: **the part of her that is reliving something over and over is angry at that situation, as if she is seeing something that doesn't actually exist anymore**).

I also had the sense that her legs were organically all right, or rather, that the source of her inability to walk was not itself organic. I understand that her legs may be damaged at this point because of the lack of use of them. (Actually, now I believe that her body is no longer structurally capable of sustaining walking.)

Having said that, I have no advice to offer except that it would be

Profoundly light-hearted strategies for unsticking stuck stuff

good if she could hold a different image of what it means to be whole. There is deep energy here needing to be released. My instinct is that this is a woman who would benefit from forgiveness training, learning the power of forgiving herself, forgiving her past, forgiving others, etc. It would also be helpful if she could separate the energy of her anger from its images or content.

If the anger is fueling her, perhaps it would be helpful if she could take that energy to a different level where it is just energy, which could be channeled in a variety of positive ways. This way it is not "angry energy," or, anger directed at someone or something in a hurtful manner (or at herself in a hurtful and essentially victimizing manner).

This would be like a public performer using the energy of stage fright to actually fuel a good performance by separating the energy from fear images of what could go wrong just by feeling and grounding the energy itself. I often have to do this, as even with over forty years of public speaking under my belt, I still get nervous every time I start a lecture or workshop.

Helping others to find wholeness through her Spine Workshop could be a wonderful way for her to go, too. I think you're on the right track here with her. Thanks for sharing her story.

I share the stories about Kat and Camilla as experiences that have taught me deeply. They illustrate my deepening understanding that our best work continually invites healing at the deepest levels of identity, even though healing may not come out looking like we want it to or thought it might. A death, approached with dignity, grace and forgiveness, can be a healing.

This isn't the stuff of one-minute wonder headlines, but I believe it *is* the stuff of the evolution of consciousness.

I continue to explore the fascinating idea that David introduced: the possibility that when healing doesn't seem to "work" that the person could somehow be "living two lives at once, this one and a previous one, like running a tape loop that has gotten stuck." That statement could easily apply to Kat in the first story too. I have that same sense of her.

I would like to learn in my work how to help people to incarnate fully and completely into this life-that-they-inhabit-now, somehow sealing the boundary between this and that other life, silencing that other voice and containing it in its own healing context. I don't know what this actually "means," but it feels intuitively right to me.

Standing up for Your Self:
the Earth is Calling YOU

CAMILLA

Camilla had been gaining weight, and was now having a hard time finding attendants who can lift and transfer her from her wheelchair. She said angrily, "I am just eating for pleasure and rebellion against having this body and this life, and having worked so hard—and *it didn't matter.*"

Out of the blue, I asked her a question that lives in me, too:

"So, if your soul is dreaming this life of yours as a way to bring something specific to the earth, what quality or capability would it want you to be manifesting?"

The question threw her into an altered state, and she said right

Profoundly light-hearted strategies for unsticking stuck stuff

away, without second-guessing herself, "Living out this body to understand its limits."

I asked her to imagine that she was
the Soul of the World.

I didn't specify what I meant by this, I just said it. Even though she had a basic distrust of spirituality and is "angry with God" for giving her this body, she trusts me, and over time has become more open to my use of weird questions and statements like this.

I asked her to BE the Soul of the World. I asked Camilla to imagine being the Earth herself speaking, as if she were "calling to herself" the life forms and patterns and energies that she, the World, needed, in order to grow and expand and deepen.

I invited her to imagine that the World *wanted and intended* to fully open toward what she was meant to be, in the same way that a person might take on an intention to deepen and grow.

The intention would be the same for a person, or the World, to draw to her or himself the experiences that would catalyze evolution toward manifesting the most joyful, creative, powerful, interesting, free, and loving life possible.

As the Soul of the World, I asked, what was her purpose in calling this particular being, this woman with these challenges of physical disability, anger, self-hatred? What would a world want from incarnating a being like this? How could a world benefit from having *her*, specifically, here?

She said slowly, thoughtfully, "It has something to do with a network, a connection, crossing paths with other beings, being a delivery vessel. It is about waking people up, opening them. I get to make people's perspective better." She doesn't usually speak this way. She sometimes says these ideas, but with anger. This was softer, a spilling out of possibilities.

I loved that idea of being a "delivery vessel!" Camilla sought some way to make her life worth living. Her deepest positive intention was to **stand up**, spiritually, from within. I thought of what David Spangler has said about this sense of Standing, with a capital S:

Standing!

How simple an act, yet how profound.

Standing embodies that inner act through which we move to a co-creative boundary between order and chaos—or for that matter, to any co-creative boundary between two or more different states of being.

Consider that when I stand, I immediately place myself in jeopardy of falling. When I am lying down, I do not fear that I will fall to the ground. I am already there! But standing puts me precariously on two feet and two legs up above the earth. Falling is now possible.

When I stand, I am at the boundary between falling (chaos) and uprightness (order). I cannot take standing for granted in the way I can when I am prone. Standing requires work; my muscles are active holding me upright. It demands attention and balance on my part. I am engaged with my world in a way I am not when I am lying down. There is a dynamic tension here that is co-creative, filled with energy.

When I stand, I put myself into a relationship with the world that is energetic, risky, and co-creative. When I stand in my individuality, I also place myself into a similar relationship with the world.

Standing is a profound spiritual act. It manifests our inner power, our inner grace, our inner alignment and balance.

It is a foundational act, from which other acts of movement and manipulation can emerge.

It is Spirit, the sacred, taking form.

THE 8 MASTER KEYS TO HEALING WHAT HURTS

" - > ` } ° ^ ° > °   > V i » °

If we can fully appreciate all that is involved, all that is invoked and evoked, just by this simple act, we might not need any other spiritual exercise.

" ^ ° ° ^ > ` ° ^ °   ° L i ° ° i ° « i ^ i V i °
v ° ^ > V i ` i ^ ^ ° >  ` ° ° V > ° ° « > V « > °
°> ° i i } } ° V ^ ^ »

(David Spangler, "Standing in Mystery," online class text)

❋ ❋ ❋

It is a good question—that one about "What is your Soul Dream? It is powerful and evocative to imagine *being* the World and inviting your own Self to come to be part of Life here.

7 > ° ` i ^ ° i °  ` ° > °   ° v ¶ ° °

9 °] ° i ° 7 ` ° V > ‰  ° L i ° v  ° >  ` °
V « i i ° ^ i v °   ° i ° > ^ v > °
> ° 9 " 1 ° L }

❋ ❋ ❋

Working with the question

Here is how you might work with this question within yourself, or with a client:

Profoundly light-hearted strategies for unsticking stuck stuff

THE 8 MASTER KEYS TO HEALING WHAT HURTS

❀ First, *be* in your own body—get present, take a moment to just be in your life, doing what you do, going where you go, feeling your usual responses to people and events, both positive and negative, as you live your life in the World as you.

❀ Let a part of you drift out of you, off to the side. In an Observer Position, watch yourself, without judgment, move through your life.

❀ Drift up to a higher overview, and take the position of a wise mentor, a guardian angel, a "higher self."

❀ Look through the eyes of someone who knows your weaknesses and your strengths, and completely loves you, wants only the best for you, honors and respects you.

❀ Ask: **What is the Soul Dream of this person that I am watching? What is the deepest yearning that shapes this person's life?**

❀ Find yourself floating down now, and in some way that feels right and is appropriate for you, imagine that you are *becoming* the World itself.

❀ Take a moment to appreciate this perspective.

❀ Now, imagine that you can sense something of the consciousness of the world as if it were an evolving being, itself, a citizen of its own community in the cosmos, with challenges of its own, yet filled with a powerful, loving, willing intention to learn how to integrate all of its richness and dramatic diversity into a harmonious symphony.

❀ *Be* the World, and watch that "human identity" going through life.

❀ Imagine that you, the World, are calling that person purposefully to you, to be part of you, to incarnate here in order to express the specific quality or story that is contained in their Soul Dream.

✳ Ask: How does that person, in all the richness of who they are, benefit and add to you, the World, in a way that *only* they could?

✳ How does their Presence honor and awaken something in the life of the World?

✳ What images, words thoughts, feelings, intuitions come to you as you hold these questions inside?

Of course, there are no right or wrong answers to these questions, just your answers.

✳ Come back into your own body, see from your own eyes, hear from your own ears, feel your own feelings.

✳ Consider the wisdom you have gained from these different perspectives.

✳ Notice and tap for any "tail enders" that pop up: the "Yes, buts..."

✳ Tap for living your Soul Dream.

,i > } i°   ° v i

✳ ✳ ✳

Some final thoughts
on love and anger and change....

Noodling around in my computer files, searching for an article I *knew* I had saved somewhere, I came across another story that I wrote many years ago about Anaiah, my tap-dancing daughter you read about in Chapter 15.

Profoundly light-hearted strategies for unsticking stuck stuff

Reading this other story and remembering the incident brought me to tears. When I sent it to her, asking if I could use this one, too, she wrote back with permission and a lovely cascade of memories and realizations of her own.

Isn't that the way it goes, like John Lennon pointed out: you find what you need while you are busy looking for something else...

Riddles

I was sitting on my eleven year-old daughter's bed as she wound down, getting ready for sleep. She was telling me some riddles that her teacher had given the class to figure out.

One of them was the one about the blue house which is one story high, the red house which is two stories, and the green house which is three stories, and you're supposed to answer the question, what color are the stairs in the blue house. I guess I wasn't paying full attention, because—too late—I heard myself say, "blue stairs." After chortling at my dumb response, Anaiah asked if I knew any riddles.

I launched into the only story riddle I could think of, one I used to tell my classes when I was a community college teacher in Chicago a long time ago:

"A father and his son were driving down the road. They got into a terrible accident. The father was killed, and the boy was rushed to the hospital. The surgeon came into the emergency room, took one look at the boy and said, 'I can't operate on that boy. He is my son.' How can that be?" (Part of telling the story is to explain that there is some legal restriction against a surgeon operating on a family member. I don't know if that is actually true).

Anaiah tried gamely to figure the riddle out. The father wasn't really killed? He came back to life? The surgeon was the boy's uncle? His grandfather? I tried to get her to picture the scene, and think what could be different about it. She came up with lots of creative ideas, but none of them made it possible for the surgeon to have said, "I can't operate on this boy. He is my son."

After awhile she got frustrated, and then she started to get mad when I wouldn't tell her the answer. She wanted to tell this riddle to her class tomorrow, but she wanted to know the answer first. It didn't seem useful for her to be mad, so I offered hints and made suggestions. Finally her eyes flew open wide and she sat up and said, "I get it! The surgeon was his *mother*!"

With a smile fired by the joy of sharing with my own daughter the power and passion of twenty-five years of feminism, I leaned toward her and said, "Yes. The surgeon was a *woman*."

Anaiah stared at me for a moment, stunned, and then burst into tears. In dismay, I gathered her to me and held her for a long time. We rocked back and forth together as she cried deep, shuddering sobs. "You *scared* me, " she said. "The look on your face *scared* me." As she cried into my shoulder I tried to figure out what was going on. Motherhood and womanhood hung in the balance here. The very air around us bristled with a still, bright, silent charge.

Even though just about everybody I know, including me, has gotten tripped up by this riddle, I was surprised that she hadn't figured out the answer. All her life I have taken her and her sister to woman doctors, dentists, chiropractors, introduced them to women who are out there in the world expressing their vitality and creativity, and seized the "teachable moment" during conversations and life events and TV shows.

Having me for a mother, she has a pretty good model of a woman doing her best to balance both active and receptive energies. And Anaiah herself often comments indignantly on sexism. However, it would seem, in this moment, that the conditioning in our culture had overcome all of that.

I tried to imagine being inside Anaiah and looking out from her eyes at me, watching and listening as I said "The surgeon was a woman" with that smile.

Suddenly, I understood.

Speaking low through her sobs, I said, "Let me tell you what I think is happening, and you let me know if it feels right to you. You are used to knowing me as your loving, hugging, helping Mom, somebody you love a lot, even though sometimes you get mad at me.

"But just now you saw a different side of me, the power in me. You are not used to seeing that, and it scared you. Maybe that power even reached into you and touched something there that hadn't been quite awake yet in you, but it got awakened a little, and that was scary too."

She kept nodding her head, buried in my neck.

I told her how I had learned about that power.

That I first learned about it through
discovering my anger.

Then I learned that my anger really did
affect people. People became very hurt and sad
when I directed my anger at them.

But until I noticed that, I hadn't experienced myself as
having very much power at all.

And then there came a time, I said, when I had to learn how to let go
of that anger, and learn how to express power through love.

I learned that feelings of anger and of love come
from the **same energy**, but you always have a **choice** about
which **way** you are going to express it.

I asked her to remember a time when she had gotten really mad.

She thought of a big argument she had had with her friend, and said, her eyes narrowing, "This was my *favorite* time of being mad at her." (Mmm, I thought, that one will work.)

Then I asked her to let go of that, and feel the love she has for her dog, and then the love she feels for me.

She could sense the powerful energy behind both love and anger. They even seemed to come through the same parts of her body, she noticed, touching her chest and wiggling her fingers. But they felt different.

> Anger makes things feel separate.
> Love makes everything feel connected.

"Where does that power come from?" Anaiah said, just about recovered from her crying now, and engaged in this conversation. "What is it usually used for in your body? Is it like the power you use for running or jumping?"

I thought that was a pretty interesting question. I really had to reach for an answer.

I told her I didn't know for sure, but I thought that this power was like your deepest essence, really what made you alive and able to act in the world. That it was a gift, and decisions about its use were the most important decisions you could make.

She was yawning now, and the moment had passed.

As I sat there in the dark holding Anaiah's hand, staring at the small glow of her clock, I thought hopefully about systems theory. How, when even the smallest change is introduced, the whole system alters to adapt to this change.

I thought about the woman Anaiah is becoming. I thought about woman-ness. Human-ness.

And I thought about the power of love.

AFTER-AFTER WORDS

I had been on the telephone all day working with Angela—the designer and my beloved midwife of this book—on the final details, when a small miracle happened. I received the following email from Leila (who you know from her stories in this book).

A couple of weeks earlier, Leila and I had shared a deeply moving EFT telephone session in which Leila—for the *very first time*—was able to return, in memory, to the actual moment when her baby was shot, and be able to be present with love and compassion with that dreadful situation in a transformative way.

LEILA

Dear Rue,

On this Easter long weekend I finally did something that has taken me years to be ready for. Yesterday, Marie, my Al Anon sponsor and friend, and I travelled to the cemetery where my little baby was buried 23 years ago.

We found his tiny gravesite in a beautiful spot—a special area set aside for unmarked children's graves. I lay down on the grass and curled around him. It felt so wonderful.

I never expected to find him in such a beautiful spot—I was prepared for it to be open and unsheltered and even bleak. Instead, it was

Profoundly light-hearted strategies for unsticking stuck stuff

sheltered by some ornamental plum trees and a big old juniper bush and some tall cedar trees. He and all the other little children there are sheltered from the storms and shaded from the summer sun.

All these years I've known that his spirit is free and whole and everywhere, but it was so comforting to find that his little earthly body has had such a safe home. I could feel his happiness. He always was happy and perfect, right from the moment he was born.

> Finally I can feel that happiness and perfection,
> instead of the horror.

The work that you and I did together made that possible. It was so incredible how neither one of us knew what we were doing ! We just let the energy of the moment help us stumble our way through until the right thing came to us. I am so amazed at how that worked. Your energy plus my energy and the two of us trusting the universe to guide us.

So now when I think of the baby I see his precious self, with the most beautiful golden line so perfect from the front of his head to the back. I see him laughing and glowing like a perfect flower. It is more beautiful than I could have ever imagined.

So thank you again Rue - I know that you and I 'facilitated' this amazing 'happening' by being willing to be guided.

> I feel so blessed.

Sending love across the continent in your direction always - Leila

I responded:

Leila—what a lovely and profoundly moving account.
What a privilege it is to share this whole healing experience with you.

Thank you from my heart, full of love and wonder.

Speaking of trusting the universe and being willing to be guided, you will be interested to hear this: when your email came, I was on the phone with the designer of this book (which has turned into *three* books, it was so long!!). (She is in Hawaii, the marvels of modern technology!)

As you know, your story is in the book (you are Leila, and I have changed/omitted some of the details to protect your identity). I mention that your baby was shot, but not the situation.

We had literally just *that very moment* finished editing the last story in the book. While Angela was making a change in the design, I heard the ding of a new email coming in, went over to to look, and there was your message.

The last line in this last story, and the book, is "And I thought about the power of love."

Your email was in Perfect Timing. As if Spirit was saying, "...and now hear this Truth about the possibility of transforming any situation into being held with love."

I'm thinking that your account of this final healing moment with you and your child is meant to be the ending of this book, to which you have already contributed so much. May I include it (with any changes that you request, of course)?

Or is this too tender a moment to be shared? I will understand if you choose not to have it used, and I am still so awed and grateful to be part of the story.

With my deep love and blessing --

Rue

Yes, dear Rue,

I trust you to use my words in whatever way you think will help others.

> If it weren't for energy psychology
> I'd still be stuck in negative
> emotions and pain.

Could you change my Al Anon counselor's name to Marie? She has been such a steadfast friend to me and supported me through thick and thin.

Nowadays when I get upset or complain about something she says, "Leila!! Remember!! Tap Tap Tap !! *Even though I feel upset and angry, I DEEPLY and completely love and accept myself !!!!*"

She thinks that my work with you has been nothing short of a miracle—she says, "Your Higher Power sure is looking after you!!"

She is very old-fashioned, so when SHE reminds me to use EFT it is so funny—it proves that you CAN teach an old dog new tricks !!

Love from Leila

THE CONTRIBUTORS

My deepest gratitude to the following people and their dedicated, excellent work.

❊ **Dr. Elisabet Sahtouris:** internationally known evolution biologist, futurist, author and professor teaching sustainable business and globalization as a natural evolutionary process. Member of the World Wisdom Council and a fellow of the World Business Academy. Venues include The World Bank, Boeing, Siemens, Hewlett-Packard, Tokyo Dome Stadium, Australian National Govt, Sao Paulo's leading business schools, State of the World Forums and the World Parliament of Religion.

Author of:
EarthDance: Living Systems in Evolution
Biology Revisioned (w. Willis Harman)
A Walk Through Time: From Stardust to Us
Sahtouris.com (professional)
Ratical.org/lifeweb (personal w. writings)

❊ **Betty Moore-Hafter:** Certified Hypnotherapist (NGH); Certified as a Regression Therapist (IBRT); Certifications in Past Life Regression, Medical Hypnotherapy, Emergency Hypnosis, Reiki, Psychosynthesis, and Spirit Releasement Therapy. Personally trained in the Emotional Freedom Technique (EFT) by its founder, Gary Craig.

Author of: "*Tapping Your Amazing Potential with EFT—* i> i°
'i>^°> '°/i>V }°/ ^° ^ }° > ° ii' °/iV i°> '°
Vi« ^°v ° « i >«."
RisingSunHealing.com

✳ **Joan Hitlin:** MFA, CCHT: energy therapist, hypnotherapist, life coach—26 years experience helping clients & students reclaim their mojo. JoanHitlin.com or Mojotivity.com

✳ **Dr David Lake:** Originator of Provocative Energy Techniques (PET) with Steve Wells. Medical practitioner: counselling & psychotherapy in the northern Sydney. Travels with Steve Wells teaching seminars in Advanced EFT and Provocative Energy Techniques (PET). Significant experience in treating trauma, use of EFT in relationship issues.

Author of: *Strategies for Stress*, the relationships manual, *She'll Be Right*; with Steve Wells: *New Energy Therapies*, and *Pocket Guide to Emotional Freedom*
EFTDownUnder.com

✳ **Steve Wells:** Psychologist, professional speaker and peak performance consultant based in Perth, Western Australia. Teaches and consults worldwide with elite athletes and corporate personnel to improve their performance and enhance the performance of their teams. Certified Speaking Professional (CSP) award from the National Speakers Association of Australia and 2004 Professional Speaker of the Year (Western Australia).

Co-authored 3 books with Dr. David Lake (see above), and *Rose and the Night Monsters* (with Jo Wiese).
EFTDownUnder.com

✳ **Poet David Whyte**: Takes his perspectives on creativity into the field of organizational development in American and international companies. Holds a degree in Marine Zoology; traveled extensively, including working as a naturalist guide; leader of anthropological and natural history expeditions. Brings wealth of experiences to his poetry, lectures and workshops.

Author of: *The Heart Aroused: Poetry and the Preservation of the Soul in Corporate America; Crossing the Unknown Sea: Work as a Pilgrimage of Identity*. Many Rivers Press 1992
ManyRiversPress.com

✳ **Dr. Kyra Mesich**, PsyD. Specializes in helping sensitive adults and children through holistic psychotherapy in St Paul, MN. Dr. Mesich's work has focused on natural remedies for sensitive people. Material in this book reprinted with permission from Dr. Kyra Mesich.

Author of: *The Sensitive Person's Survival Guide.*
KyraMesich.com.

✳ **Alison Luterman**: HIV counselor, drug and alcohol counselor, drama teacher, freelance reporter; has taught poetry workshops in schools.

Poet, essayist, short story writer and playwright. Her pieces have appeared in publications * i ° > ^] °* i °   i] °7 i ^   i] ° >   « i] °"L i] °/ -] ° ^ >   ] °/ i °   °,i i] °* i °   i] ° >   Her first book, "*The Largest Possible Life*" won the Cleveland State University Poetry Prize 2000 and was published in the Sun Magazine in2001.
See more poems here: oldpoetry.com/authors/Alison%20Luterman and plagiarist.com/poetry/4391/

✳ **David Spangler:** Writer, philosopher and teacher of spiritual perspectives. "Incarnational Spirituality is the foundation for all of Lorian's work. It is an affirmation of the spirit innate within our world, our humanity, our physicality, and our personal lives. It sees each person as a source of spiritual power and radiance. Incarnational Spirituality is grounded in our sovereignty as individuals. Each of us is a unique incarnation of sacredness able to make contributions that no one else can make to the wellbeing of our world and the positive unfoldment of our future."
Lorian.org

✳ **Ananga Sivyer:** Energy Healing researcher 20 years, specialising in Meridian Energy Therapies, Energy Psychology, and Personal Development. She is a Licensed Trainer and Director of The Association for Meridian Energy Therapies, NLP Practitioner and guest presenter at the European Energy Psychology Conference. Contributing health editor and columnist for **Lifescape Magazine**
Author of: The Art & Science of Emotional Freedom, a workbook.
Ananga.squarespace.com

❋ **Silvia Hartmann:** Author of: *"Adventures In EFT and Advanced Patterns of EFT"*
SilviaHartmann.com

❋ **Angela Treat Lyon:** Artist, Author, Book Designer/Creator, Success Coach, EFT Practitioner, Rocket Fuel Tool inventor, Trainer trainer. A radical gal who loves to see people take hold of their lives and run for all they're worth into a glorious play of outrageous success, health and wealth.

Author: *The Real Money Secrets Book; Change Your Mind! with EFT; Six Little P.I.G.E.E.S. Learn the Amazing Money Multiplying Methodde; 9 Secrets to Writing Blockbuster Books.*
AngelaTreatLyon.com, EFTBooks.com, PIGEES.com.

❋ **The Tiger:** I got the image of the tiger in the cage about forty eons ago, and have no idea where I got it from, or who the artist is. I searched online for the artist, and came up with the original photo it was sourced from—but no artist. If you know who painted this, please contact me so I can give the artist full credit and appreciation! Thanks! And may your inner tiger always feel like the one on the right (illustration by Angela Treat Lyon)!

❋ ❋ ❋

❋ Rue Anne Hass, M.A., EFT Master

Master EFT Practitioner, intuitive mentor/life path coach in Madison, Wisconsin since 1986 using "profoundly lighthearted strategies for unsticking stuck stuff."

A long time ago, I was a college English teacher. From being a teacher I learned about how to learn, how to think about what was important, and how to communicate that clearly. I also learned that people in positions of authority are given respect whether they deserve it or not, and I set an intention for myself to deserve the respect I was given.

This was in the 1960's and early 70's, a time of a great creative ferment in the US and the world. I found myself in the center of this paradigm shift, deeply involved in the women's movement and the anti-war movement, living in an urban commune in Chicago that shared income, child care and household tasks. My job in our group was to take care of the household automobiles. (I was also teaching auto mechanics in a women's educational cooperative). From the experiences of this time I learned a sense of agency: that I had a place in the world, that we are all part of a bigger picture, that what I did and thought mattered.

From 1974-1981, I was a staff member of the Findhorn Foundation, an international center for spiritual and holistic education in Scotland. Here, I was deeply challenged to learn and experience my own spiritual truth, independent of spiritual teachers and what other people said were the prerequisites for spiritual progress. I learned to surrender my prickly anger and the sense of personal "power over" in order to open to love and "power with".

Since then, I credit much of what I have learned in life to the bright enchantments and difficult challenges of motherhood and marriage. My daughters are now in their 20's, beautiful young women from the inside out. I am profoundly honored that they set me up with their friends for counseling/coaching sessions when I visit them. One is an acupuncturist in Denver, Colorado, and the other is in marketing in Boston, Massachusetts. I married Timothy at Findhorn. He works for an outpatient psychiatric unit, plays soccer, and would meditate all day if somebody paid him to. I think of him as a "mystic jock."

I have extensive training in psycho-spiritual philosophy and therapies. Today, EFT is the centerpiece of my work. In January, 2006 I was honored to be named the 14th EFT Master. I love the simplicity and effectiveness of EFT, and the fact that it is a tool that people can take home with them. They don't always have to be going to the "expert" to get "fixed" because they are "broken." Now we have healing at our own fingertips!

What really powers me in my life is an intense curiosity about consciousness and a deep love of the world. I think of myself as a "Wise Woman in Training." (I have no intention of graduating! I will always be in training.)

In a first meeting with a new client/co-creative partner, I might walk them through an interesting process of understanding their life as a story, that I describe as "mapping the history of your future." It concludes with asking you to consider: "What do you want your life to leave in the world as a legacy. How do you want the world to be a better place for your having been here?"

I ask myself this question. What emerges for me is fostering in every way I can imagine, at all times, to my best ability, the concept of "Wealthbeing." This term popped into my head one day when I was thinking about the process of manifestation. To me, Wealthbeing means an interesting synthesis of "well-being" and "being (instead of having) wealth." I invite and assist people and communities to move into a sense of the real transformative power of their Wealthbeing, their own specific spiritual Presence in the world.

If you read this book, you can probably tell that I am inspired by the work of David Spangler (*Everyday Miracles*; *Parent as Mystic/Mystic as Parent*; *Blessing: the Art and Practice*):

" ....each of us is a collaborative participant in the unfoldment and co-creation of the world. We are each direct links between the primal creative act – the Word from which all things spring – and the world in which we live our daily lives.

We are embodiments of that Word and we speak it in our own unique ways through our lives.

This speaking of the creative Word is the essence of a new emerging 'incarnational spirituality.' We can experience the empowerment of spirituality as support for our ordinary lives, integrating us into the world, based on the sacred in the personal rather than only the transpersonal."

Profoundly light-hearted strategies for unsticking stuck stuff

THE 8 MASTER KEYS TO
HEALING WHAT HURTS
by © Rue Hass 2005
protected by International Copyright Laws

Rue@IntuitiveMentoring.com

Cover design, editing, book design and construction
by Angela Treat Lyon

Published by
/U T & R O N ŒR O D U C T IO N S
Kailua, Hawaii 96734
808-261-0941
Lyon@AngelaTreatLyon.com